mental math
Challenges

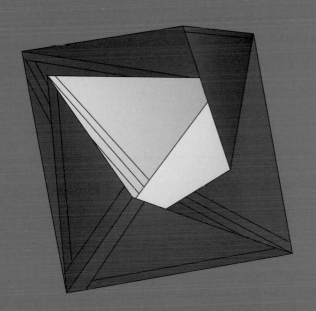

Michael L. Lobosco

Sterling Publishing Co., Inc. New York

A Sterling/Tamos Book

A Sterling/Tamos Book
© 1999 Michael L. Lobosco

Sterling Publishing Co., Inc.
387 Park Avenue South
New York, NY 10016-8810

TAMOS Books Inc.
300 Wales Avenue
Winnipeg, MB Canada R2M 2S9

10 9 8 7 6 5 4 3 2 1

Distributed in Canada by Sterling Publishing Co., Inc.
c/o Canadian Manda Group, One Atlantic Avenue, Suite 105
Toronto, Ontario, Canada M6K 3E7
Distributed in Great Britain and Europe by Cassell PLC,
Wellington House, 125 Strand, London WC2R 0BB, England
Distributed in Australia by Capricorn Link (Australia) Pty Ltd.
P.O. Box 6651, Baulkham Hills, Business Centre,
NSW 2153, Australia

Design A. O. Osen
Photography grajewski•fotograph.inc

Printed in China

Canadian Cataloging-in-Publication Data
Lobosco, Michael L. (Michael Louis), 1918–
        Mental math challenges
        "A Sterling/Tamos book."
        Includes index.
1. Mathematical recreations. I. Title.
QA95.L622 1999 793.7'4 C98-920155-4

Library of Congress Cataloging-in-Publication Data
        Data available.

ISBN 1-895569-50-8

2

Acknowledgments
A special thanks to my daughters, Maria Porcella Rowe and Diana Strom, and their husbands, Barry Rowe and Ivan Strom, for their help with the text and graphics of this book. I also gratefully acknowledge the following people whose ideas I shared or revised for some of the activities in this book: James T. Anderson, Barnabas Hughes, J. F. F. Pearcy, K. Lewis, Harold R. Jacobs, and my son Angelo for his constructive criticism. I dedicate this book to my wife, Jennie, whose patience and understanding allowed me many uninterrupted late-night hours during which I was able to complete the research necessary to finish the book.

Note Power tools and sharp objects are used in some projects. Children should ask an adult for help.

Contents

Introduction   **4**

Beauty With Circles and Flexagons   **5**
Floating Sphere   **6**
3-D Stadium Design From Concentric Circles   **9**
Tetraflexagon—An Unusual Flexagon   **13**
Transforming Magical Shapes   **16**
Tetrahedron Makes a Terrific Paperweight   **18**
Mind-Boggling Flexatube   **20**

Instant Calculations and Mind Reading   **23**
Amazing Number 143   **24**
429 Product Reveals Chosen Number   **26**
Hyakugo Gen—Famous Japanese Formula   **27**
The Confident Gambler   **28**
Amazing Prediction of Top Card in Addition Triangle   **30**
The Odd King's Odd-Numbered Problem   **33**
Choose Your Fortune Mind-Reading Feat   **34**
Split-Second Multiplication by Cutting Strip   **39**
Lightning Addition   **40**
Add Five Items Faster Than a Calculator   **41**

Vanishes and Illusions   **43**
The Case of the Missing Dollar   **44**
Another Case of the Missing Dollar   **45**
Toothbrush Changes Color in a Flash   **47**
2—3 Prong Illusion   **48**
65 Squares, 64 Squares, 63 Squares   **50**

Precision Measuring Without Instruments   **51**
Measuring Small Round Objects With a Paper Micrometer   **53**
Precise Line Measurement With a Diagonal Scale   **54**
Measuring the Height of a Flagpole With a Mirror and Yardstick   **55**

Math in Everyday Life Situations   **56**
The Smart Greek's Formula and the Road Builder's Dilemma   **57**
Two Squares Always Make a Larger Square   **59**
Solve Algebra Problems Instantly With Geometry Card   **60**
How Many Paths Can You Take to Spell Your Name   **62**
The Many Different Paths From John's House   **65**
Find the Area of This Unusual Garden   **66**

Solitaire Games   **68**
Lucky Seven   **69**
Twenty Triangles Make a Perfect Square   **70**
Moving Nine Pennies in Nine Moves   **71**
Buffon Toothpick Experiment   **73**
Japanese Very Different Tangrams   **74**
Make a Square With Only Five Pieces   **77**
Create a Perfect Star and Play the Numbers Game   **78**

Index   **80**

Imagine making a perfect sphere with only straight line segments of silvery thread, or guessing a friend's age with three simple questions, or adding a total of five random shopping items faster than a calculator, or changing a pink toothbrush to blue in an instant. Impossible? No, quite possible and easy by learning a simple math idea! These math miracles and many more can be yours with a little practice and help from this book.

Learning math is not a spectator sport. It's a fun activity of doing, thinking, and experimenting. The aim of **Mental Math Challenges** is to give you unusual math ideas through a wealth of different hands-on tasks and do-it-yourself activities using simple materials and inexpensive supplies. These ideas take math out of the paper-and-pencil class and make it something more than manipulating numbers in a workbook.

The projects in this book are not expensive to construct. Everyone has access to the materials. You can use recycled materials from cardboard boxes and cartons, blocks and plywood from lumber yards, and discarded manila folders from banks and stores. Items such as toothpicks, string, nails, rubber bands, tape, dowels, and sandpaper—all things you probably have in your home—can be used to make projects that are fun to do, surprisingly beautiful, mysteriously magical, and richly satisfying.

This book, in fact, offers you action workouts for mental alertness and well-being. You'll find complete directions to make working models for a variety of math puzzles. All you need to participate is time, effort, and patience. The rewards are many. You can create new designs and shapes, or discover a new strategy to cope with a demanding situation, or find a surprising answer to a mystifying challenge. But more importantly, these mental workouts will hone your mental abilities towards a more logical and reasonable way of thinking.

Try these challenges and you'll find that math is exciting, creative, and rewarding in ways that you never expected.

Beauty
With Circles and Flexagons

FLOATING SPHERE

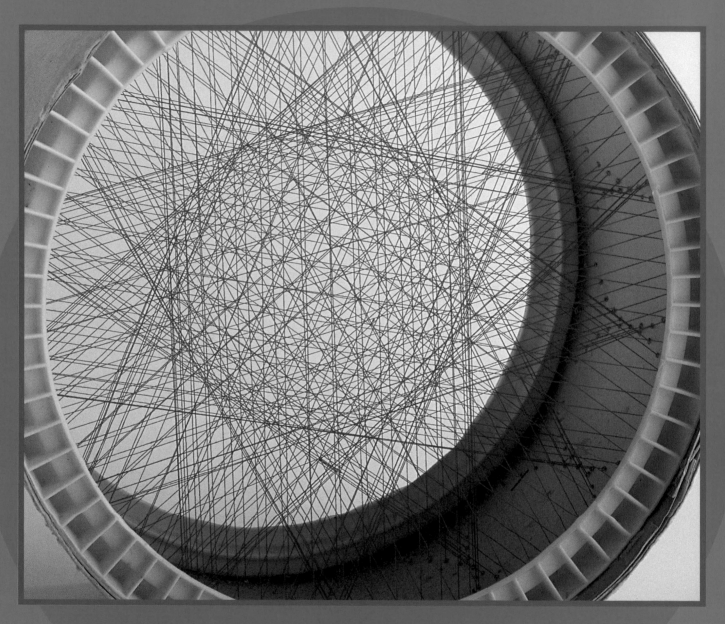

Have you ever seen a floating sphere—one constructed of line segments and built within a cylinder? It is difficult to visualize and almost impossible to draw; but it can be constructed with careful effort. Try it and experience an exciting miracle illusion combining math and art. This construction in space mathematics is one of many geometrical architectural designs possible. It is called aestheometry, and this floating sphere construction is credited to James T. Anderson.

MATERIALS NEEDED
6-ply bristol board, 4 in x 22 in (10.2 cm x 55.9 cm)
circle pattern, page 8
awl or tack pin
medium size needle
3 spools of red no. 50 mercerized thread
masking tape
scissors
pencil
stapler

CONSTRUCTION

1 Photocopy pattern on page 8 and cut out.

2 Draw a line along the center length of the bristol board. Leave a 1 in (2.5 cm) margin on one end of the board. Draw two more lines **a** and **b**, as shown.

3 Lay the pattern on the board.

4 Using the pattern, draw circles on the center line, as shown. Number the circles from 1 to 14.

5 Use a pencil and draw a point every 10° around each circle, as indicated on the pattern.

6 With an awl or tack pin, punch out every 10° point marked.

Note Every 30° point from the top of each circle should coincide with the 330° point of the following circle.

7 Staple the ends of the bristol board

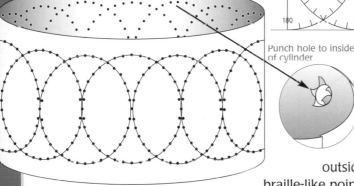

Punch hole to inside of cylinder

to form a cylinder. Be sure to connect the two half circles at the ends of the pattern into one circle making fourteen circles in all. The drawn pattern will be on the outside of the cylinder and the braille-like points on the inside.

8 Thread the needle with at least 8 feet (2.4 m) of thread. Tape the end of the thread to the outside of the cylinder in the middle of circle #1. Do not tape over the holes in the pattern.

9 Start from the 90° mark of circle #1. Push the needle through this hole and cross the center of the circle to the other side. Push the needle through the cylinder at the 90° mark of circle #6.

10 Skip two circles around the outside of the cylinder to circle #8 and push the needle and thread back into the cylinder through the 90° mark of #8. Cross the interior of the cylinder parallel to the first crossing and exit the cylinder at the 90° mark of circle #13. Skip three circles around the outside to circle #2, and enter the cylinder at 90° mark of #2. Cross the center of the cylinder to #7. (Each crossing skips five circles.) Exit, skip two circles to #9, then enter, cross to #14, then skip three circles to #3, cross to #8, etc. Repeat the pattern of cross, skip two, cross, skip three, cross, skip two, etc., until a circle formed by the thread is completed.

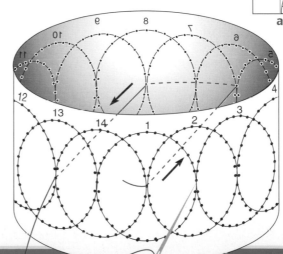

1 in (2.5 cm)

Pattern is—enter circle #1, cross to #6, skip two circles to #8.

> #8 cross to #13, skip three to #2.
> #2 cross to #7, skip two to #9.
> #9 cross to #14, skip three to #3.
> #3 cross to #8, skip two to #10.
> #10 cross to #1, skip three to #4.
> #4 cross to #9, skip two to #11.
> #11 cross to #2, skip three to #5.
> #5 cross to #10, skip two to #12.
> #12 cross to #3, skip three to #6.
> #6 cross to #11, skip two to #13.
> #13 cross to #4, skip three to #7.
> #7 cross to #12, skip two to #14.
> #14 cross to #5, skip three to #8.
> Repeat #8 cross to #13, etc.

11 To string the next circle begin at circle #1 again, at the hole next to 90°. Continue the pattern as before, using the next row of holes.
Note The thread enters the cylinder *to the left* of the 90° hole, but exits at the other side *to the right* of the 90° hole (as viewed from the outside). This causes the string to cross itself just inside the cylinder. It also produces progressively smaller circles in the center, which is what eventually forms the sphere.

Note Build the floating sphere away from the center on both sides of the cylinder.
(Do not pull the threads too taut causing the cylinder to lose its shape. Threads may be tightened when the center circle is completed. Working on alternate sides helps to prevent the cylinder from becoming lopsided during construction.)

12 When stringing is completed, cover the outside of the cylinder with a suitable colored or designed paper to hide the holes, tape, and threads. Hang near a window, look through your work and enjoy the illusion of a beautiful, floating sphere in the cylinder.

CHALLENGE

Make other patterns using different stringing sequences.

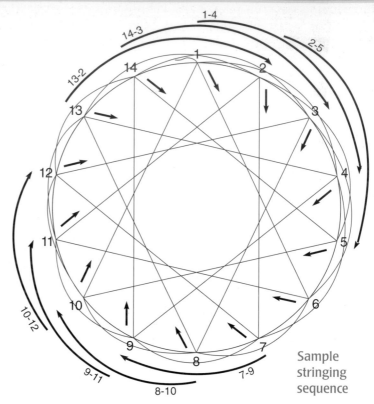

Sample stringing sequence

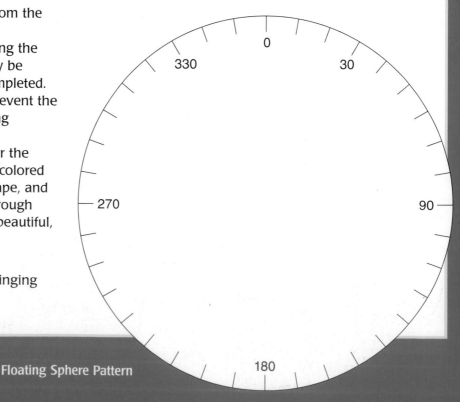

Floating Sphere Pattern

3-D STADIUM DESIGN
from concentric circles

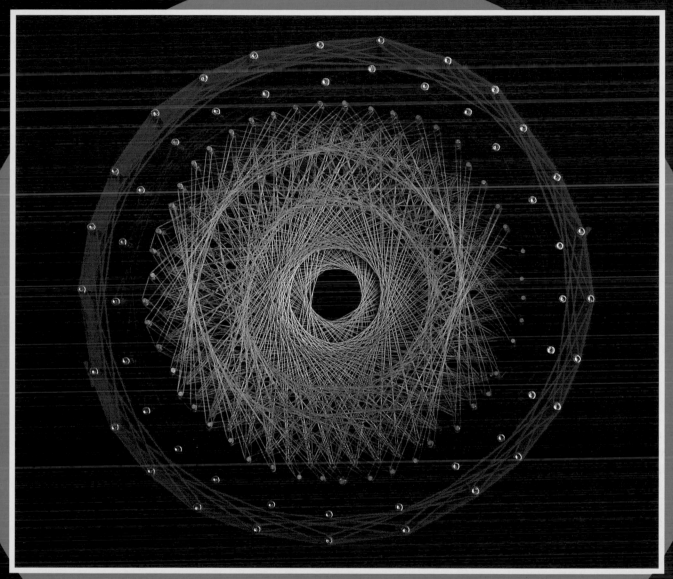

Have you ever tried to draw a design with a continuous pencil stroke without retracing the pencil's path and without lifting the pencil from the paper? Let's make an intricate and beautiful design with at least three concentric circles, but instead of a single stroke of the pencil, the construction will use a single thread for each circle! You can connect twenty-four nails to each other for each circle and never retrace the thread!

Another attractive design, suitable for a wall hanging, can be constructed in a similar manner with three different dimensions on a flat surface.

MATERIALS NEEDED
cloth of your choice, 14 in x 14 in (35.6 cm x 35.6 cm)
wood board, 8½ x 10 in (21.6 cm x 25.4 cm)
24 brass or steel nails, 1½ in (3.8 cm) in length
48 brass or steel nails, 2½ in (6.4 cm) in length
4 different colored threads (half spool of each color)
hammer
stapler
pattern, page 12
scissors

CONSTRUCTION

1 Cover the board with the material. Staple excess material on the back of the board.

2 Photocopy the pattern on page 12. Cut out. Note You can enlarge the pattern to the design size desired.

3 Place this pattern on the cloth-covered board, and hammer 1½ in (3.8 cm) nails on the 24 points of the circle.

4 Remove the paper and, using one thread color for each diagram, begin stringing, as shown.

Diagram A   Stringing sequence

Using pink thread, move thread from nail 1 to 12; go back to nail 1, making a double strand. Then move thread to nail 2 and go to 13; again double back to 2. Then move thread to nail 3; 3 to 14. Again back to 3; 3 to 4; 4 to 15; back to nail 4; then to nail 5, etc., until you reach nail 24. Repeat the sequence: 1 to 12; 12 to 1; 1 to 2; 2 to 13; 13 to 2; 2 to 3; 3 to 14; 14 to 3; 3 to 4, etc., until you reach nail 24.

Diagram B   Stringing sequence

Using blue thread, move thread from nail 1 to 10; back to 1; 1 to 2; 2 to 11; back to 2; 2 to 3; 3 to 12, etc. until you reach nail 24. Stringing sequence B creates a larger circle than stringing sequence A.

The diagram at lower right shows the colors combined for stringing sequence A and B colors, as they would appear in this project. Sequence B is created on top of sequence A when doing the actual project. For clarity the colors are kept separate in the diagrams.

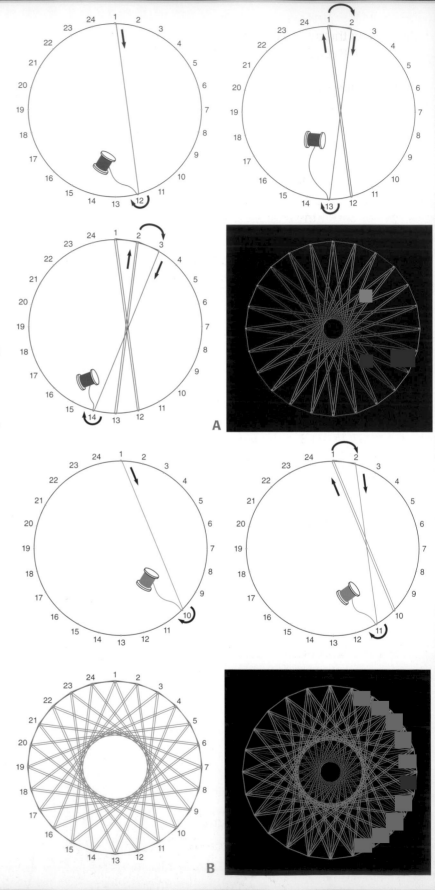

A

B

Diagram C Stringing sequence

Using yellow thread, move thread from nail 1 to nail 8; back to 1; 1 to 2; 2 to 9; 9 to 2; 2 to 3, etc. until you reach nail 24. Stringing sequence C creates the largest circle in the pattern.

The diagram at C (right) shows the colors combined for stringing sequence A and B and C colors, as they would appear in this project. Sequence C is created on top of sequence A and B when doing the actual project. For clarity the colors are kept separate in the diagrams.

Note To create a fourth tier with a fourth color, you may start by skipping five nails. 1 to 6; 6 to 1; 1 to 2; 2 to 7; 7 to 2; 2 to 3; 3 to 8, etc. When you reach nail 24, you have completed the fourth tier.

5 For the stadium wall, hammer two rows of 2½ in (6.4 cm) nails around the outside of the design. The first row of 24 nails should have each nail ½ in (1.3 cm) away from the first row of nails making a circular wall ½ in (1.3 cm) wide.

The completed wall may be strung with a different color string.

C

CHALLENGE

You have constructed many diagonals in making this polygon-shaped stadium. Can you figure how many different diagonals an N-sided polygon has?

Hint We know that a three-sided polygon (triangle) has 0 diagonals, a four-sided polygon (square) has 2 diagonals, a five-sided polygon (pentagon) has 5 diagonals, and a six-sided polygon (hexagon) has 9 diagonals.

Can you discover the rule for N-sided polygons? Draw some polygons and construct diagonals in them and look for a pattern. Don't give up! See solution, page 12.

EXTRA CHALLENGE

The diagonals from each point of a twenty-four-sided polygon touch only nine points of that polygon.

How many diagonals are there?

The twenty-four-sided polygon at right (M) shows a different stringing sequence. Can you discover the pattern used?

M

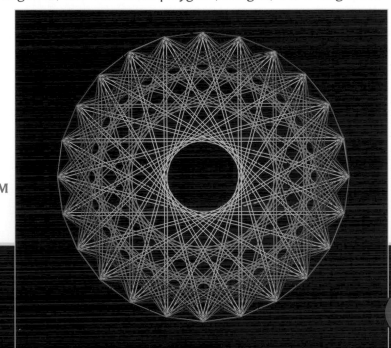

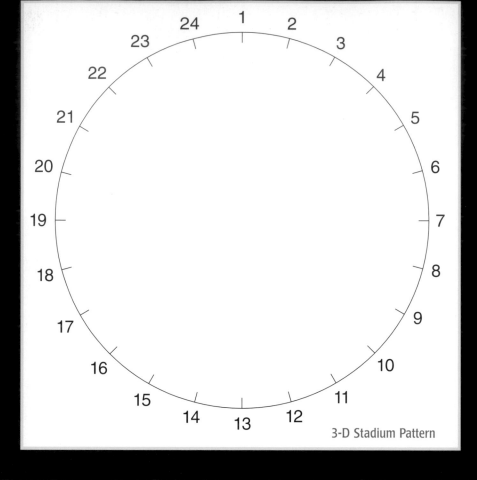

3-D Stadium Pattern

Solution to 3-D Stadium Design from Concentric Circles

Challenge

No. of sides	No. of diagonals	No. of sides	No. of diagonals
4	2	8	20
5	5	9	27
6	9	10	35
7	14	n	$\frac{n(n-3)}{2}$

As sides of the polygon increase by 1, the increase from the previous number of diagonals increases by 1.

Extra Challenge

See M, page 11. Nine diagonals have been drawn from each point (1 to 3, 1 to 4, 1 to 5, . . ., 1 to 11, 2 to 4, 2 to 5, etc.). It appears that eighteen diagonals come off each point (from 1, from 2, etc.). But at point 1, the first nine diagonals do start from point 1, the other diagonals start at points 15, 16, 17, and end at point 1. This is the same for all other points. Since diagonals would be counted twice, the total is 24 x 18 divided by 2 = 216.

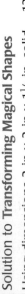

Solution to Transforming Magical Shapes

Using dimensions 3 in x 3 in x 1½ in, solid = 13½ cu in (7.6 cm x 7.6 cm x 3.8 cm, solid = 219.5 cu cm)
Smaller pyramid is ⅙ size of larger solid so divide volume by 6 = 2.25 cu in or 36.6 cu cm.

TETRAFLEXAGON
an unusual flexagon

Imagine producing six different designs with a flick of the wrist. This variation of the more common hexaflexagon forms these distinct colorful arrangements by inverting symbols and figures on squares. A little effort in constructing will reward you with a fascinating project combining art and geometry.

MATERIALS NEEDED
heavy paper, 12 in (30.5 cm) square
scissors
ruler
markers or colored pencils
tape

CONSTRUCTION

1 Using ruler and marker, divide the large paper square into sixteen smaller squares, each 3 in (7.6 cm) square.

2 Fold sheet along marked grid lines, and cut out the four center squares, leaving a frame of twelve squares, four on each side, as shown.

3 Beginning at the upper left corner of this frame, number the squares on both sides of the frame in the order shown. To make the folding process clearer, each side of the paper in the illustrations has a different color.

4 Fold each of the three sides of the frame inward, one at a time, toward the center, as shown.

5 Tape, as indicated, to make assembly easier.

6 Now grasp the double square 1, pull it forward, invert it, and tuck it under the last 2 to complete the flexagon.

7 Remove the tapes.

8 On the squares behind the four 2s there should be four 5s, if the flexagon is assembled correctly.

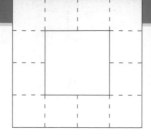

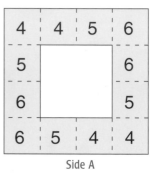
Side A

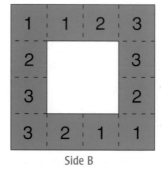
Side B

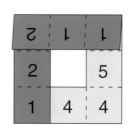
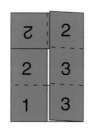
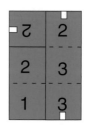

If assembled correctly
Side A and B

9 The flexagon can now be made quite interesting by placing different colors and designs in each of the numbered surfaces. The flexagon can be flexed up or down, right or left, to create twelve different artistic combinations and unusual surprises.

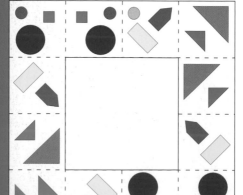

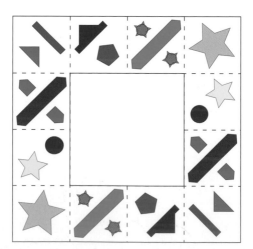

14

Flexing the Flexagon

Color the flexagon and create designs, as desired. Hold the flexagon with square or color No. 1 at the lower right corner. Close the flexagon as you would a book, and open from the bottom. Repeat the same move: close and open again to reveal the first four colors or designs. Reverse the closing and opening moves two times to return to original starting position.

Now, turn the flexagon one quarter turn clockwise. Close the flexagon like a book again; open from the bottom and a fifth new color or design will appear. Repeat the closing and opening move again and the sixth color or design will appear. Reverse the last two moves and the flexagon will be ready to start the entire sequence of designs again.

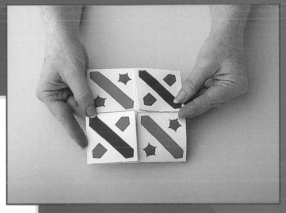

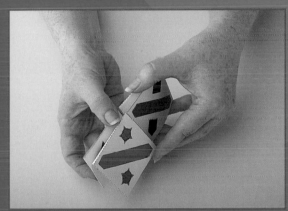

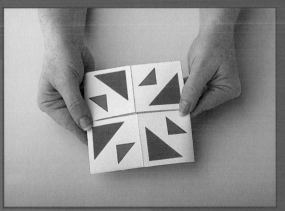

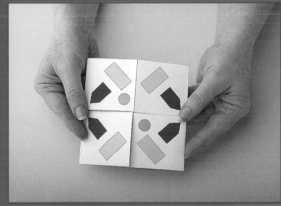

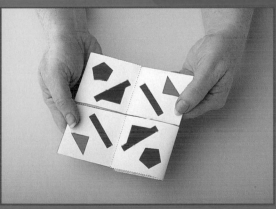

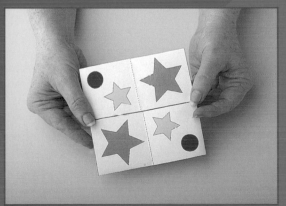

transforming
MAGICAL SHAPES

Take a square base solid and four rectangular base solids, cut, fold, and stick the sides together to form five pyramids, then quickly arrange and tape in a row to make three pyramids. Then tape each pair of the smaller shapes in a clever manner, and, like magic, produce a rectangular solid. Like magic, five pyramids change to three identical pyramids that transform into one rectangular solid.

MATERIALS NEEDED
heavy paper or oak tag
utility knife
ruler
pencil
tape

CONSTRUCTION

1 Enlarge and photocopy the two patterns onto the heavy paper. Make one square base pyramid (pattern 1) and four smaller pyramids (pattern 2).

2 Cut out on the solid lines.

3 Score and fold on dotted lines to construct one pyramid with a square base and four smaller pyramids with rectangular bases. Tape edges of each pyramid to make three-dimensional shapes.

4 Tape to form a row of three pyramids, as shown.

5 Tape the smaller pyramids in a unique fashion to enable the transformation of all shapes into a rectangular solid, as shown below.

CHALLENGE

What is the volume of the rectangular solid?

What is the volume of the smaller pyramid?

See solution, page 12.

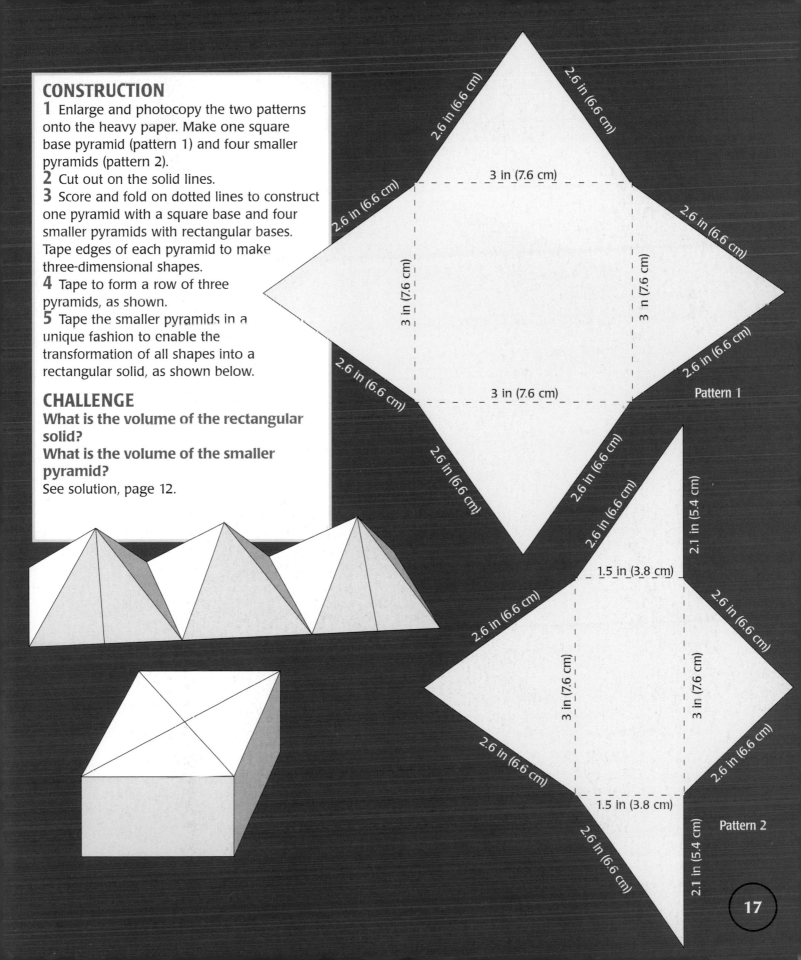

Pattern 1

2.6 in (6.6 cm)

3 in (7.6 cm)

3 in (7.6 cm)

3 in (7.6 cm)

3 in (7.6 cm)

Pattern 2

1.5 in (3.8 cm)

2.1 in (5.4 cm)

3 in (7.6 cm)

3 in (7.6 cm)

1.5 in (3.8 cm)

2.1 in (5.4 cm)

2.6 in (6.6 cm)

17

TETRAHEDRON
makes a terrific paperweight

Four triangles and a parallelogram can create a tetrahedron. The pattern has four flaps that fold inside the figure to give it stability. When the triangles and parallelogram are folded they form a three-dimensional shape that is exactly one quarter the size of a perfect tetrahedron.

MATERIALS NEEDED
2 standard letter size sheets heavy paper or oak tag
pattern, page 19
scissors
ruler
heavy coin or iron washer
tape
glue
silver paper foil or colored paper

CONSTRUCTION

1 Photocopy the pattern onto half a sheet of heavy paper or oak tag. Each side marked should equal 2 in (5.1 cm). Two patterns will easily fit on each sheet. Make four pattern copies.

2 Cut on the solid lines and score on the dotted lines for easy assembly.

3 Fold on the dotted lines and tuck in the four tabs on each pattern. A small strip of tape on one corner will keep the shape quite firm.

4 Once all four identical shapes are completed, use the shapes to form a tetrahedron.

5 Glue the coin or iron washer to the base and cover with red paper or paper with an original design and color of your choice.

CHALLENGE

The challenge is to tape the shapes in a very logical manner to form a perfect tetrahedron. Though difficult, your efforts will be rewarded with a beautiful paperweight when the project is completed.

Hint The hard way is to assemble these pieces in a random manner. A logical procedure eliminates hundreds of trial-and-error steps. Can you find it? See solution, page 22.

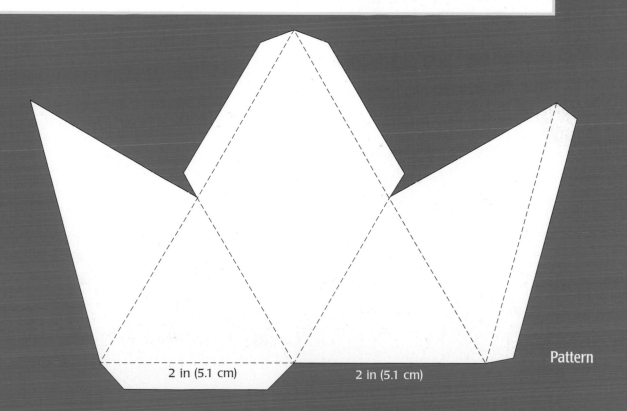

2 in (5.1 cm)   2 in (5.1 cm)   Pattern

mind-boggling
FLEXATUBE

This simple, yet intriguing flexagon, is in the form of a cube with no top or bottom. Each of the four square sides can be folded along two diagonals. Once the performer learns the folding secrets, he or she can invert this tube, almost magically, without forcing in any way, to produce the inside design or color in a matter of seconds.

MATERIALS NEEDED
heavy cardboard or thin plywood
masking tape or duct tape, 1 in (2.5 cm) wide
utility knife or saw

CONSTRUCTION

1 Cut four squares of cardboard or thin plywood, 2½ in x 2½ in (6.4 cm x 6.4 cm).

2 Divide each square into quarters by drawing its two diagonals and cutting along the diagonals, as shown. You will have four triangles from each square, or sixteen in all.

3 Lay four triangles to form each square, ¼ in (0.6 cm) apart.

4 Tape them so that the triangles of each square can flex and fold upon each other easily.

5 Then tape them into a rectangular strip, also ¼ in (0.6 cm) apart.

6 Tape ends of the strip to complete the flexatube.

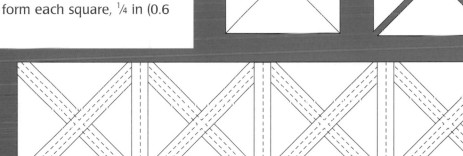

¼ in (0.6 cm)

Note To create a different color for the inside of the flexatube:
  If using cardboard, glue two different colors together, back to back, before cutting squares into quarters.
  If using thin plywood, paint one side a different color, before cutting squares into quarters.
  Or use colored pencils or markers to decorate the pieces before assembling.
It is more difficult to color the pieces after they are taped together.

Flexing the Flexatube

1 Flatten the cube to make a square.

2 Fold this square to make a triangle shape. Look into this triangle and see two folded triangular flaps.

3 Now flatten this triangle into a smaller square. Bring the right and left corners together, but at the same time, make sure that one of the folded flaps folds forward and the other folds to the rear.

4 Form a small rectangle from the square just formed by inserting a finger in the front pocket of the square, and another finger in the back pocket of the opposite side of the square. Pull the fingers apart to form the rectangular tube, as shown. You have now turned half of the tube inside out.

5 Perform every previous step in reverse order. The small inverted tube can easily be unfolded into the small square. The small square opens up to form a triangle, which quickly opens up to form a larger square. Open up the square to reveal the inverted flexatube!

With a little practice you can learn to flex this flexatube in seconds!

Solution to Tetrahedron Makes a Terrific Paperweight
Knowing that each shape has the same volume (one quarter of the tetrahedron) the most logical procedure is to somehow construct half of the tetrahedron first. That is, tape together two of the four shapes. If at first two halves cannot easily be assembled into a tetrahedron, re-form the halves and try again. When you have formed the halves to fit correctly, it will be a fairly simple matter to assemble the perfect tetrahedron. Trying to fit the individual quarters together one at a time would be a most difficult task!

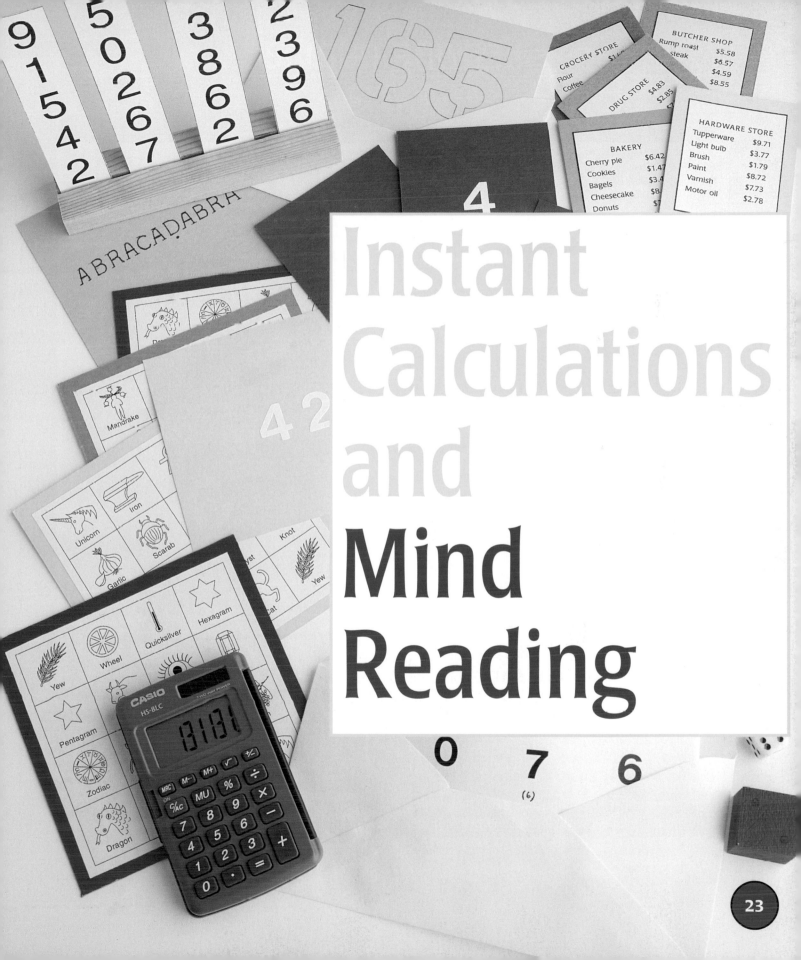

Instant
Calculations
and
Mind
Reading

amazing number
1 4 3

This little known, but amazing number 1 4 3 can make you a master calculator if you know the magic secret. First, place the digits 1, 4, 3 on the table before a friend. Ask your friend to give you any three-digit number to multiply this magic number by. You then immediately write the answer beneath the chosen number. Have the friend verify the answer with a calculator.

MATERIALS NEEDED
4 pieces of heavy paper or cardboard, each 3 in (7.6 cm) square
magic marker
calculator

CONSTRUCTION

1 Using the square cards write the numbers 1, 2, 3, and 4 on them. On the backs of 1, 3, and 4, place dots (1 dot on 1, 3 dots on 3, 4 dots on 4) so that you can easily identify them. Leave the back of card 2 blank.

2 To perform the magic calculation, mix the four cards and place them face down noting which cards have the marks on them. Ask the friend to select one of the four cards. If the friend selects card 2, quickly gather the remaining three cards and turn them up in this order–1 4 3. Point out that this is the magic three-digit number.

3 If the friend chooses 1, 4, or 3, pick up card 2 and place it aside and ask the friend to give you the remaining two cards face down. Then, noting the marks on the backs, turn them up in order to make 1 4 3. Designate this as the magic number.

4 Place the cards in order on a piece of paper, as shown. Ask a friend to choose a three-digit number.

Examples Friend chooses 917.
Place 917 under 143 and
multiply:

```
      143
    x 917  (think 917917 and
   131131      divide it by 7)
        131131
     7)917917
```

Friend chooses 246.
Place 246 under 143 and
multiply:

```
      143
    x 246  (think 246246 and
    35178      divide it by 7)
        35178
     7)246246
```

CHALLENGE

Why does dividing by 7 into the chosen number repeated always produce the correct answer?

Hint 143 x 7 = 1001

Solution to **4 2 9 Product Reveals Chosen Number**

The two basic numbers to remember are 250 and 9. Assume the die number is 1–think 250 and 9. 1 x 250 = 250; 1 x 9 = 9. 250 + 9 = 259. 259 X 429 =111111.

Assume the number is 2. Again think 250 and 9.
2 x 250 = 500; 2 x 9 = 18; 500 + 18 = 518. 518 x 429 = 222222.
If number is 3–think 3 x 250 = 750; 3 x 9 = 27. 750 + 27 = 777.
777 x 429 = 333333.
If number is 4, 4 x 250 =1000; 4 x 9 = 36. 1000 + 36 = 1036.
1036 x 429 = 444444.
If number is 5, 5 x 250 =1250; 5 x 9 = 45. 1250 + 45 = 1295.
1295 x 429 = 555555.
If number is 6, 6 x 250 =1500 6 x 9 = 54. 1500 + 54 = 1554.
1554 x 429 = 666666.

Solution to **Amazing Number 1 4 3**

Take any three-digit number times magic number 1 4 3. Example 642. If three 0s are added to 642, the answer is 642,000. 642,000 is obviously 1000 x 642. Add 642 to get 642,642. This also is obviously 1001 x 642. But we don't want to multiply 642 by 1001. We want to multiply 642 by 143 (the magic number). Consider this little-known fact: 143 is $\frac{1}{7}$ of 1001. Therefore, to do the magic calculation you multiply any number (in this case 642) by 1001 by repeating as above: 642,642. Then take $\frac{1}{7}$ of it (the same as multiplying it by 143).

Divide by 7:

```
        91806
    7)642642
```

642 x 143 = 91806

4 2 9 PRODUCT
reveals chosen number

Triple the amazing number 1 4 3 from the previous activity and create another very unusual number: 4 2 9. Have a friend enter 429 in a calculator. Then ask the friend to roll a die for a number. Assume it is 4. Immediately have the friend multiply 429 in the calculator by a certain number and it instantly reveals 444444!

MATERIALS NEEDED
light cardboard, 2 in x 6 in (5.1 cm x 15.2 cm)
magic marker
wood cube, 1 in (2.5 cm) square
calculator

CONSTRUCTION
1 On the card print 4 2 9.
2 On the wood cube print the numbers 1, 2, 3, 4, 5, and 6— one on each side.

PROCEDURE
Point out to the friend that because this number 4 2 9 is triple another amazing number (143), it can produce very unusual results. Show the card with the number and have 429 entered in the calculator. Ask the friend to roll the wood cube (die) to choose a number. In this case, assume the number to be 4. Ask the friend to quickly multiply 429 by 1036 and the rolled die number appears six times: 444444. But you have already written down the answer, to your friend's amazement. Try it with another roll of the die. It may be the number 6. Tell your friend to multiply 429 by 1554 and again the rolled die number appears six times.

How do you know what number to multiply 429 by?

HYAKUGO GEN
famous Japanese formula

Ask a friend to divide his or her age by three simple numbers—3, 5, and 7, but don't give the answer, just the remainders. In any division what is left over is known as the remainder—0 or any other number. With only the remainders you can guess the age instantly. No materials or construction are needed for this project.

PROCEDURE

1 Ask your friend to divide his/her age by 3 and tell you the remainder only.

2 Ask your friend to divide his/her age again by 5 and tell you the remainder only.

3 Finally ask your friend to divide his/her age by 7 and tell you the remainder only.

4 After each question asked, take note of each remainder given and multiply first remainder x 70; multiply second remainder x 21; and multiply third remainder x 15.

5 Add these three products. As in the famous puzzle, Hyakugo Gen, subtract 105 from your answer, if possible. The result is the age of the person who gave you the numbers. If the answer, after multiplying the three remainders and adding is less than 105, simply leave the answer as is.

Examples

Assume the age to be 25

$3) \overline{25}$ with 1 as remainder (1 x 70 = 70)

$5) \overline{25}$ with 0 as remainder (0 x 21 = 0)

$7) \overline{25}$ with 4 as remainder (4 x 15 = 60)

Add 70 + 0 + 60 = 130 − 105 = 25

Assume the age to be 100

$3) \overline{100}$ with 1 as remainder (1 x 70 = 70)

$5) \overline{100}$ with 0 as remainder (0 x 21 = 0)

$7) \overline{100}$ with 2 as remainder (2 x 15 = 30)

Add 70 + 0 + 30 = 100

THE CONFIDENT GAMBLER

The confident gambler brags of his mental mind-reading skill and proposes a wager with two of his poker friends. He bets that he can read their minds. He places, face up, three sets of cards, and asks each friend to choose a set. From these cards the friends select three numbers, which, when added together, reveal a total he had already predicted in a sealed envelope that he had shown to his friends beforehand. How did the gambler do it?

MATERIALS NEEDED
deck of playing cards
envelope
light cardboard card that fits inside
    envelope
marker pen

PROCEDURE

1 Select these cards from the deck; arrange cards, like suits together, as shown, in any order.

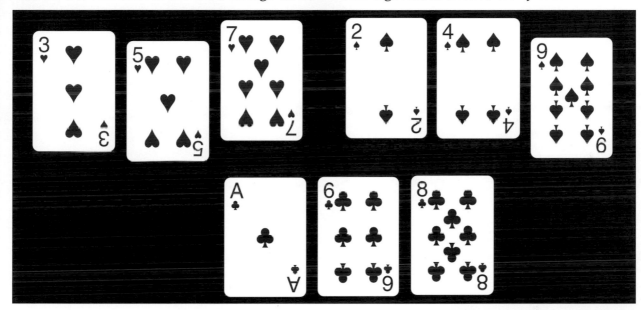

2 Write the number 165 on a piece of cardboard that fits in the envelope. Place the card in the envelope and seal the envelope. The confident gambler lays one row of three hearts, one row of three spades, and one row of three clubs on a table.

3 He asks the two friends to each choose the suit they prefer: hearts, spades, or clubs. Gambler pockets the third suit. (Assume friends choose hearts and spades.)

4 Gambler now asks player number 1 to lay down a heart card and player number 2 to lay down a spade card next to it.

5 Players 1 and 2 lay down second card each.

6 Players 1 and 2 lay down last card each.

7 Gambler totals the three numbers: 165.

8 Gambler tears open the sealed envelope with his prediction in it—165!

Why does this number prediction always work?

See solution, page 32.

assume — representing 34

assume — representing 52

assume — representing 79

amazing prediction of top card in
ADDITION TRIANGLE

This very unusual math card trick was invented by Harry Lorayne, a memory expert, using a deck of cards from which the face cards and the tens have been removed.

MATERIALS NEEDED
deck of playing cards

PROCEDURE

1 Remove 10s and face cards from deck of cards and set aside. Ask a spectator to choose five cards at random from the reduced deck.

2 The math magician places the five cards face up in a row, as shown.

3 He then selects another card and places it face down, five card lengths above this first row, as shown.

4 The magician then instructs the spectator to build a triangle of cards under the face down card by adding values as follows beginning with the row of four cards:

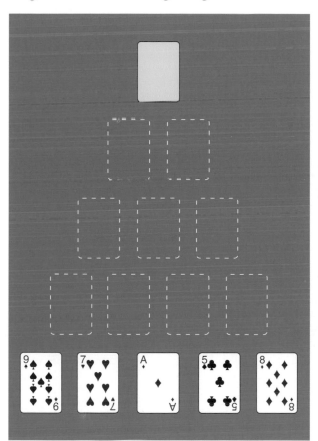

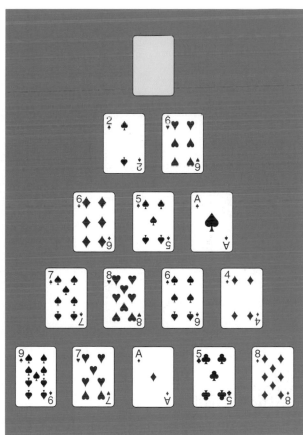

place each card that is the sum of the two cards below it. If a 7 and a 1 are below, place an 8; If a 5 and 6 are below and the sum is more than 9, either subtract 9 from the sum or add the digits of the sum. For example, 5 plus 6 equals 11. Either subtract 9 from 11 which equals 2 or add digits 1 plus 1 which equals 2. Repeat for the next two rows.

5 After all the adding is done, the face down card that the math magician has placed earlier is revealed to be an 8.

How did the math magician know to select this card?

CHALLENGE

How is this top card determined in advance, even though the first (bottom) row of cards may contain 5, 6, 7, or 8 cards?

Hint Look for a formula in Pascal's Triangle in activity The Many Different Paths From John's House on page 65.

See solution, page 32

Solution to The Confident Gambler

Gambler knows that no matter what trio of cards is chosen, the totals of the three hearts cards is 15; the three spades is 15; and the three clubs is 15. In the example illustrated:

3 ♥ and 4 ♠ – 34
5 ♥ and 2 ♠ – 52
7 ♥ and 9 ♠ – 79
165

Note The hundreds column is always 150 or 30 + 50 + 70 = 150. Also, the ones column is always 15 or 4 + 2 + 9 = 15. Add these two sums and get 165. Therefore, the answer will always be 165.

Solution to Amazing Prediction of Top Card in Addition Triangle

The Pascal Triangle is another addition triangle where each of the numbers is the sum of the two numbers above. Working downward from the row of 1s, all other numbers are the sum of the two above. (Note underlined numbers: 2, 3, 3, 4, 6, 4, 5, 10, 10, 5.)

In the Card Triangle, consider that all interior cards, also underlined, have the same value as the underlined numbers at the same position in the Pascal Triangle. Example: the 6 of hearts has a value of 2 but with a total value of 12 (6 x 2). The 5 and ace cards with values of 3 have total values of 15 and 3 respectively (5 x 3 and 1 x 3).

Quickly determine the secret card at the top by multiplying and adding the values of the cards in the bottom row. Then, if the total of the digits exceeds 9, subtract 9 to get the value of the secret card.

To solve the six card triangle arrangement (A) with 2 ♣, 6 ♥, and 5 ♣ on the bottom row: multiply face value of the three cards times 1, 2, and 1: 2 x 1, 6 x 2, and 5 x 1 and add the three amounts (2 + 12 + 5 = 19) or digit sum (1 + 9) of 10 – 9 = 1 (top card).

To solve 5 row card arrangement on page 31: ace has value of 6; cards 5 and 7 are 12 x 4 = 48; cards 9 and 8 are 17 x 1 = 17. Adding values 6 + 48 + 17 = 71. Therefore: 7 + 1 = 8, the number on the face down card.

To solve the ten card triangle arrangement (B) with 6 ♦, 5 ♠, 1 ♠, and 4 ♦ on the bottom row. Multiply face value of the four cards times 1, 3, 3, and 1 respectively: 6 x 1, 5 x 3, 1 x 3, and 4 x 1 and add amounts (6 + 15 +

3 + 4 = 28) or digit sum
(2 + 8) of 10 – 9 = 1 (top card).

To solve the card arrangement (C) of six rows with six cards on the bottom, consider the following:

The ace
♣ and
5 ♦
are

6 x 10 for a value of 60;
the 7 ♥ and 8 ♣ are 15 x 5 for a value of 75, and 9 ♦ and ace ♥ are 10 x 1 for a value of 10. Add amounts (60 + 75 + 10 = 145) or a digit sum (1 + 4 + 5) of 10. 10 – 9 = 1 (top card).

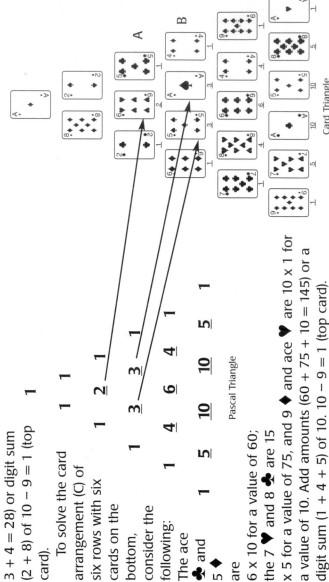

Pascal Triangle

```
            1

        1       1

    1       2       1

1       3       3       1

1   4       6       4   1

1   5   10      10  5   1
```

Card Triangle

A   B   C

the odd king's
ODD-NUMBERED PROBLEM

An ancient fable tells of a king who had a beautiful twenty-year-old daughter. But he also had a phobia for odd numbers, so when her many suitors wanted to win her hand in marriage, the King posed a problem for them to solve. Each suitor had to arrange exactly eight odd-numbered cards which, when added together, would produce a sum equal to the age of his daughter. To simplify this task, each suitor could use any eight of the odd-number cards from two complete decks of cards (jacks represent 11 and kings 13).

MATERIALS NEEDED
2 decks of playing cards

PROCEDURE

1 Select 8 each of 3s, 5s, 7s, 9s, jacks, kings, and aces. Set the rest of the decks aside.

There are only three ways to add four odd-number cards to get the sum of 10.

$$1 + 1 + 3 + 5 = 10$$
$$1 + 1 + 1 + 7 = 10$$
$$1 + 3 + 3 + 3 = 10$$

But there are many more than three solutions to get 20, and to get them all you need to be systematic. The king said that all solutions had to be found! One solution is shown below.

See additional solutions, page 38.

choose your fortune
MIND-READING FEAT

What will your fortune be? Select a charm, but don't tell the mind reader. Through his or her magical powers of deduction your selection is identified and your fortune is revealed. How is this done?

MATERIALS NEEDED
heavy cardboard sheet, approx. 16 in x 19 in (40.6 cm x 48.3 cm)
5 oak tag or heavy cardbord cards, 5 in x 6 in (12.7 cm x 15.2 cm)
several sheets of bond paper
scissors
paper
pencil
glue

Crystal	Unicorn	Iron
Opal	Lodestone	Frog
Topaz	Garlic	Diamond

Rowan	Emerald	Knot
Beryl	Mandrake	Verbena
Amethyst	Ankh	Cat

Charm Patterns

Pentagram	Scarab	Dragon
Horseshoe	Bull	Nail
Wheel	Jade	Quicksilver

| Hexagram | Eye | Zodiak | Yew |

CONSTRUCTION

1 Photocopy all charm patterns, enlarging to the desired size.

2 Cut out individually and paste on large piece of cardboard.

3 Photocopy the five small charm cards (pages 35–36) and paste onto the five oak tag cards.

4 On the back of each of the five small charm cards, write the word ABRACADABRA.

5 On the back of card A, place 1 small dot under the A; on card B, place 1 small dot under the B; on card C, place 1 small dot under the C; on card D, place 1 small dot under the D. Card E will have no dots. See diagram, page 37.

Unicorn	Iron	Ankh	Mandrake
Garlic	Scarab	Crystal	Emerald
Eye	Opal	Amethyst	Knot
Quicksilver	Wheel	Cat	Yew

Charm Card A

Dragon	Zodiac	Garlic	Ankh
Rowan	Eye	Opal	Beryl
Crystal	Nail	Jade	Frog
Wheel	Knot	Verbena	Scarab

Charm Card B

Mandrake	Frog	Opal	Verbena
Cat	Bull	Topaz	Garlic
Lodestone	Eye	Emerald	Wheel
Dragon	Diamond	Nail	Unicorn

Charm Card C

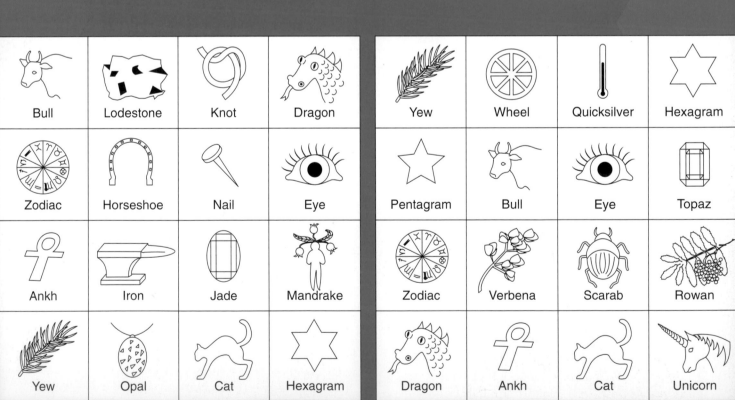

Bull	Lodestone	Knot	Dragon
Zodiac	Horseshoe	Nail	Eye
Ankh	Iron	Jade	Mandrake
Yew	Opal	Cat	Hexagram

Charm Card D

Yew	Wheel	Quicksilver	Hexagram
Pentagram	Bull	Eye	Topaz
Zodiac	Verbena	Scarab	Rowan
Dragon	Ankh	Cat	Unicorn

Charm Card E

To perform the mind reading

After a favorite charm is pointed out behind the performer's back, the performer hands out the five cards to one or more spectators to look for the chosen charm. The spectators retain the cards with that charm on it, and lay the others on the table. The mind reader casually picks up the discards, then concentrates on the person who chose the charm, and quickly writes the name of the chosen charm! He then checks the Magic Charm List and gives the person's fortune. To learn how the trick is done, see page 38.

ABRACADABRA	ABRACADABRA	ABRACADABRA	ABRACADABRA	ABRACADABRA
Charm Card A	Charm Card B	Charm Card C	Charm Card D	Charm Card E

MAGIC CHARM LIST

1 **Amethyst** (choosing this sign you will never drink to excess)
2 **Beryl** (you will have a good marriage)
3 **Crystal** (you have the gift of seeing into the future)
4 **Diamond** (you can heal breaches of friendship)
5 **Emerald** (you will have clear sight)
6 **Frog** (this is a love charm)
7 **Garlic** (scares away sorcerers)
8 **Horseshoe** (for luck)
9 **Iron** (drives away demons)
10 **Jade** (for long life)
11 **Knot** (helps true love)
12 **Lodestone** (attracts love)
13 **Mandrake** (procures good fortune)
14 **Nail** (for luck)
15 **Opal** (bestows the gift of prophecy)
16 **Pentagram** (powerful protection against bad luck)
17 **Quicksilver** (prevents jaundice)
18 **Rowan** (keeps bad luck away)
19 **Scarab** (protects against evil)
20 **Topaz** (for a contented mind)
21 **Unicorn** (can detect poison with its horn)
22 **Verbena** (makes you irresistible)
23 **Wheel** (helps misfortune to roll by)
24 **Hexagram** (controls evil spirits)
25 **Yew** (symbol of continuing life)
26 **Zodiac** (worn on a ring for luck)
27 **Ankh** (the Egyptian symbol of life—a T with a circle on top)
28 **Bull** (a fertility symbol)
29 **Cat** (lucky, especially if black)
30 **Dragon** (a popular Chinese amulet for longevity)
31 **Eye** (an anti-witch talisman)

Solution to The Odd King's Odd-Numbered Problem

As in packing your car trunk, start with the large items and work down. You can't use 19, 17, or 15 because they don't leave room for seven more odd numbers and you don't have cards for them.

Starting with 13, it is possible to add seven 1s for the answer.

$$13 + 1 + 1 + 1 + 1 + 1 + 1 + 1 = 20$$

Starting with 11, you can't use 9, 7, or 5. Try 3:

$$11 + 3 + 1 + 1 + 1 + 1 + 1 + 1 = 20$$

No other solution with eight odd numbers added to 11 is possible.

Starting with 9, you can't use 7 because $9 + 7 = 16$, and there are no six odd numbers that add to 4, so use $9 + 5$:

$$9 + 5 + 1 + 1 + 1 + 1 + 1 + 1 = 20$$

You can now use 9 and two 3s:

$$9 + 3 + 3 + 1 + 1 + 1 + 1 + 1 = 20$$

By trial and error, using smaller odd numbers, the seven other solutions are:

$$7 + 7 + 1 + 1 + 1 + 1 + 1 + 1 = 20$$
$$7 + 5 + 3 + 1 + 1 + 1 + 1 + 1 = 20$$
$$7 + 3 + 3 + 3 + 1 + 1 + 1 + 1 = 20$$
$$5 + 5 + 3 + 3 + 1 + 1 + 1 + 1 = 20$$
$$5 + 5 + 5 + 1 + 1 + 1 + 1 + 1 = 20$$
$$5 + 3 + 3 + 3 + 3 + 1 + 1 + 1 = 20$$
$$3 + 3 + 3 + 3 + 3 + 3 + 1 + 1 = 20$$

Solution to Choose Your Fortune Mind-Reading Feat

Performer knows that each charm represents its own number, alphabetically: amethyst = 1, beryl = 2, crystal = 3, etc. up to zodiac which is 26. Numbers 27 to 31 represent life symbols – ankh, bull, cat, dragon, and eye. Each card A, B, C, D, and E has number mentally assigned to it, as follows: A=1, B = 2, C= 4, D= 8, E = 16.

Example

Suppose the spectator mentally chooses "Nail." He will keep cards B, C, and D (on which nail appears), and discard cards A and E which total $1 + 16$ or 17. Subtract this from 31. The answer is 14, which is the number for Nail. Having done this calculation, the mind reader writes Nail. Another method is to find the letter for the required number by the made-up word EJOTY. You will see that

$$E = 5, J = 10, O = 15, T = 20, \text{ and } Y = 25. \text{ Again "Nail,"}$$

discarded cards A and E = $1 + 16$ or 17. Subtract 17 from 31 = 14. Using EJOTY–14 is closest to 15 which is O in alphabet, so go down one to N. Look at charm beginning with N and you have Nail.

Solution to Split-Second Multiplication by Cutting a Strip

A cyclic number is a number obtained by changing a fraction to a decimal that repeats in cycles: for example, $\frac{1}{3}$ (1 divided by 3) = .333333 . . ., $\frac{1}{6}$ (1 divided by 6) = .166666 . . ., $\frac{2}{3}$ (2 divided by 3) = .666666 . . . The challenge number 0 7 6 9 2 3, is one of the most remarkable in our number system. It is obtained by dividing 1 by 13, which equals .07692307692307... It has this unusual property–when multiplied by numbers from 1 to 12, the product contains the same digits of two numbers: 076923 (the original number), and 153846 (the product of seven prime numbers–2, 3, 3, 3, 7, 11, and 37).

Note the products, from 1 to 12, and in the same order.

1 x 076923 = 076923	4 x 076923 = 307692	7 x 076923 = 538461	10 x 076923 = 769230
2 x 076923 = 153846	5 x 076923 = 384615	8 x 076923 = 615384	11 x 076923 = 846153
3 x 076923 = 230769	6 x 076923 = 461538	9 x 076923 = 692307	12 x 076923 = 923076

The number on the front of the strip is 076923. The digits of this number will yield the answers if the die roll is 1, 3, or 4. We multiply by 3 because the ones digit of 076923 is 3. If the die roll is 1, think 1 x 3: (3), so we cut the strip to the right of the 3 to reveal 076923. If the die roll is 3, think 3 x 3: (9), so we cut the strip to the right of the 9 to reveal 230769. If the die roll is 4, think 4 x 3: (12), and we cut the strip to the right of the 2 to reveal 307692.

For the die rolls of 2, 5, and 6, the answers are on the back side of the strip: 153846, 384615, and 461538. If the roll of the die is 2, since the numbers on the back side of the strip are not visible, when cutting through the envelope, look for the key numbers in parentheses (2), (5), and (6), in small print, under the 3, 9, and 7, as shown on page 39.

If the die roll is 2, cut to the right of small (2), to reveal 153846.
If the die roll is 5, cut to the right of small (5), to reveal 384615.
If the die roll is 6, cut to the right of small (6), to reveal 461538.

SPLIT-SECOND MULTIPLICATION
by cutting strip

This amazing multiplication feat uses a rare cyclic number: 0 7 6 9 2 3. Using only a number rolled on a die and this amazing split-second multiplication, the first six products will be found on a strip of paper prepared beforehand. This is how you do it.

MATERIALS NEEDED
paper strip, 11 in x 2 in (27.9 cm x 5.1 cm)
tape
marker
envelope (small letter size)
die
scissors
calculator
sheet of paper

CONSTRUCTION

1 Lightly fold the strip of paper in half (do not crease). On the left half of side A, using large numbers, write 0 7 6; on the right half write 9 2 3. Turn the strip over and on the left half of side B write 6 4 8; on the right half write 3 5 1, as shown. Write the small numbers in parentheses exactly as shown on side A of the strip.

2 Tape the ends of the strip together to form a loop that will fit into the envelope.

3 Place the loop in the envelope with the flap of the envelope between the two halves, as shown.

076923
(6)   (5)   (2)
Side A

153846
Side B

PROCEDURE

1 On a separate sheet of paper write the cyclic number 0 7 6 9 2 3.

2 Hand the spectator a die. Ask the spectator to roll the die to find a number. Assume the number is 3. Spectator multiplies 076923 by 3, using a calculator. The answer is 230769.

3 Tell the spectator that the answer is already in the envelope you are holding. Cut the envelope and the enclosed strip and the answer appears.

How is this done? See solution, page 38.

The math magician challenges any number of spectators with calculators to add the numbers formed by mixing the number strips any of forty-eight different ways. Before the numbers can be entered in the calculators, the magician announces the answer.

MATERIALS NEEDED
4 strips of cardboard or poster board, 2 in x 5 in (5.1 cm x 12.7 cm)
scissors
wood board, 4 in x 16 in x ¾ in (10.2 cm x 40.6 cm x 1.9 cm)
saw
marker
calculators

CONSTRUCTION
1 On each of the four strips, draw five digits, as shown, on front and back of strips.
2 Cut ¼ in (0.6 cm) groove in the wood board so the strips can stand upright. Sand and paint board, as desired.

9	5	4	2		3	1	6	8
9	5	4	2		3	1	6	8
1	0	3	2		8	5	4	7
5	2	8	3		6	4	2	1
4	6	6	9		4	7	7	7
2	7	2	6		7	8	5	4

Front   Back

PROCEDURE
Ask a friend to mix the strips, arranging them on the board in any order.

You now have five numbers running horizontally, each with four digits. The four-digit number across the top row is 9148, and the number across the next row is 1537. The other numbers are 5481, 4767, and 2824. The math wizard glances at these five numbers and announces the total sum before those with calculators can enter the numbers in their calculators. When the calculators finally do add the numbers, the total is the same as that already announced.
Can you figure out the secret for this miracle addition?

Hint The five digits on each vertical strip add to 20 something. Can you figure out what that 20 something is? Four of the five digits always add to 20.
See solution, page 42.

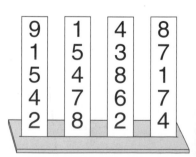

Example: one way to arrange the strips.

ADD FIVE ITEMS
faster than a calculator

An instant calculation! Have one, two, or as many as five spectators take a colored card shopping list. Any one item from each list may be chosen and its cost may be announced to someone with a calculator. No matter how quickly these prices are called out, the math magician announces the total quicker than the calculator.

MATERIALS NEEDED
5 different color cards, 3 in x 4½ in
 (7.6 cm x 11.4 cm)
white paper
scissors
glue or paste
calculator

CONSTRUCTION

1 Photocopy the five shopping lists below on white paper. Cut out each list.
2 Paste or glue each list onto a different color card.

BAKERY		BUTCHER SHOP		DRUG STORE		HARDWARE STORE		GROCERY STORE	
Cherry pie	$6.42	Rump roast	$5.58	Maalox	$4.83	Tupperware	$9.71	Flour	$1.68
Cookies	$1.47	Rib steak	$6.57	Listerine	$2.85	Light bulb	$3.77	Coffee	$6.63
Bagels	$3.45	Bacon	$4.59	Vitamin E	$7.80	Brush	$1.79	Slim-Fast	$9.60
Cheesecake	$8.40	London broil	$8.55	No-Doz	$1.86	Paint	$8.72	Cheese	$3.66
Donuts	$7.41	Top sirloin	$7.56	Advil	$3.84	Varnish	$7.73	Wisk	$5.64
Layer cake	$5.43	Veal	$9.54	Metamucil	$6.81	Motor oil	$2.78	Tea	$2.67

CHALLENGE

The price numbers on the five cards look like random numbers, but they are not random at all. They are special sets of numbers that can be added easily with a small mental calculation. Note the 10s digit of the six prices on each card. What do you also notice about the 1s and 100s digits on each price of those items?

 Try adding five items (one from each card) ten times. Record these ten dollar amounts and study them carefully. Each amount has something in common with the others.

Can you discover what makes this math magic?

Hint Almost all these amounts are four digits. Break the four digits up into two pairs.

See solution, page 42.

Solution to Lightning Addition

The first, third, fourth, and fifth vertical digits on each strip always add to 20. And the first, third, fourth, and fifth horizontal numbers will always add to 22220. 9148 + 5481 + 4767 + 2824 = 22220. Therefore, to get the answer, simply add to this number the second horizontal number 1537, as follows: 1537 + 22220 = 23757

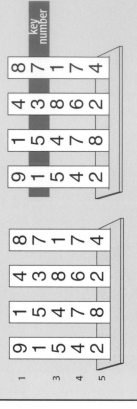

Solution to Add Five Items Faster Than a Calculator

Add five items, one from each store, for your shopping list. Let us simulate three separate shopping lists from the five cards, taking one item from each of the five stores:

	List A	List B	List C
Drug store (1st)	$4.83	$2.85	$7.80
Bakery (2nd)	6.42	1.47	3.45
Butcher shop (3rd)	5.58	6.57	4.59
Grocery store (4th)	1.68	6.63	9.60
Hardware store (5th)	9.71	3.77	1.79
Total Amounts	$28.22	$21.29	$27.23

Note the following significant similarity:

The 10s digit of the prices on the first card is always 8, on the second card it is always 4, on the third card it is always 5, on the fourth card it is always 6, and on the fifth card it is always 7.

The simple calculation for obtaining the first two digits of the total amount is: Add the final-digit penny amounts (the last digit of the five prices called out).

Note the penny amounts for the shopping lists A, B, and C (above)

Shopping list A	3 + 2 + 8 + 8 + 1 = 22
Shopping list B	5 + 7 + 7 + 3 + 7 = 29
Shopping list C	0 + 5 + 9 + 0 + 9 = 23

The second two digits of the total amount are obtained by subtracting the penny totals from 50. Note the second two digit amounts for lists A, B, and C:

List A	$28.22 (50 − 22) = 28
List B	$21.29 (50 − 29) = 21
List C	$27.23 (50 − 23) = 27

Vanishes
and
Illusions

the case of the
MISSING DOLLAR

Count forty-nine $ signs, seven in a row and seven rows. But wait! Move three of the four pieces in this puzzle and, not only does one $ sign completely disappear, leaving forty-eight $ signs, but the math magician creates an empty square that the extra $ sign had occupied. The math magician then takes a single square with a $ sign on it and places it in the empty square.

> **MATERIALS NEEDED**
> heavy paper or lightweight cardboard,
>   7 in x 7 in (17.8 cm x 17.8 cm) square
> single 1-in (2.5-cm) square piece of
>   lightweight cardboard
> patterns
> scissors
> paste or glue

Pattern B

Pattern A

CONSTRUCTION
1 Enlarge patterns to make pattern **A** 7 in x 7 in (17.8 cm x 17.8 cm) square and pattern **B** 1 in (2.5 cm) square.
2 Paste or glue the pattern photocopies on the heavy paper or lightweight cardboard.
3 Cut pattern **A** on line **ab** to form one right triangle, on **cd** and **ef** to form two trapezoids and one small rectangle.
4 Attach pattern **B** to the back of a trapezoid with tape.

PROCEDURE
Form the 7 in x 7 in (17.8 cm x 17.8 cm) square from the four pieces you have cut out putting the right triangle on the base of the square, the two trapezoids on it (small trapezoid on the left) and the small rectangle on top left corner. Leave the 1-in (2.5-cm) square piece on the back of the trapezoid. Count the $ signs (49). Now transpose the two trapezoids that rest

on the triangle allowing the 1 in x 3 in (2.5 cm x 7.6 cm) rectangle to sit on the wider trapezoid, leaving forty-eight signs and one empty square space, as shown. The math magician takes the 1-in (2.5-cm) square piece from the back of the trapezoid and places it in the empty space.

Can you explain this vanish?

See solution, page 46.

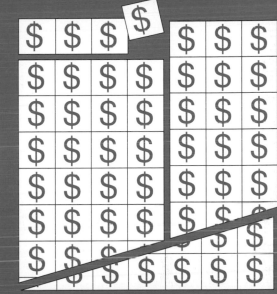

another case of the
MISSING DOLLAR

A store sold thirty oranges on sale at two for a dollar and another group of thirty oranges at three for a dollar. The first thirty sold out and brought in fifteen dollars. Later that day, the other thirty sold out and brought in ten dollars. This was a total of twenty-five dollars for all sixty.

The next day sixty more oranges were brought in to sell. The manager thought, Why bother to sort them? If thirty sell at two for one dollar and thirty more sell at three for one dollar, why not put all sixty in a pile and sell them at five for two dollars? It's the same thing.

But wait! When all sixty oranges were sold (twelve groups of five each) at five for two dollars, they brought in 12 x $2 or $24. Yesterday, sixty oranges brought in $25. **What happened to the missing dollar?** See solution, page 46.

Solution to The Case of the Missing Dollar

The dollar signs in this vanish cleverly disguise the extra dollar along the diagonal cut of the original forty-nine dollar arrangement. When the trapezoids are transposed, the irregular dollar formations along the diagonal, though they seem to fit, in reality are a little larger than the original dollars in the forty-nine dollar arrangement. This accounts for the empty space in the second arrangement.

Solution to Another Case of the Missing Dollar

On the first day thirty oranges sold at 2 for $1 or 50 cents each and the other thirty sold at 3 for $1 or 33⅓ cents each. The average price for all sixty oranges was 83⅓ cents divided by 2 or 41⅔ cents each.

But on the second day all sixty oranges were sold at 5 for $2 averaging 40 cents each or 1⅔ cents less than on the first day.

Therefore, 60 x 1⅔ ¢ = $1. This is the amount lost on the second day!

Solution to Toothbrush Changes Color in a Flash

Two brushes appear to be incomplete but that illusion makes this vanish and color change work. Seven slightly smaller toothbrushes (the striped ones on page 47 left) become six larger toothbrushes after the transposition. The same thing happens to the plain toothbrushes. When colored and accurately drawn, it is really impossible to locate the toothbrush that changes color!

46

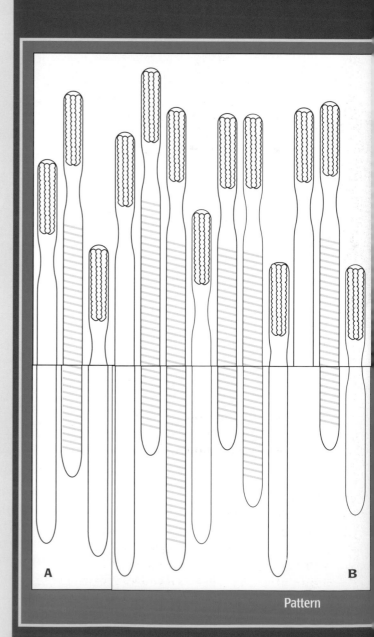

Pattern

TOOTHBRUSH CHANGES COLOR
in a flash

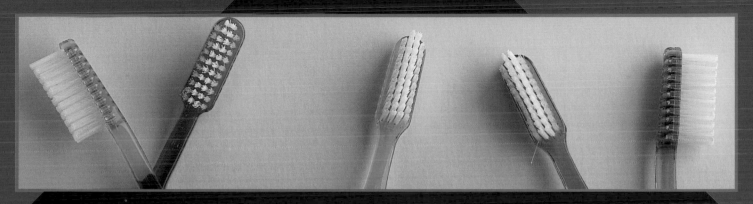

Here is an original color-changing miracle that defies logic. Thirteen toothbrushes—6 pink and 7 blue—change to 7 pink and 6 blue in an instant!

MATERIALS NEEDED
heavy cardboard, 6 in x 11 in (15.2 cm x 27.9 cm)
pattern, page 46
pink and blue magic markers
scissors
paste

CONSTRUCTION

1 Photocopy toothbrushes pattern on page 46 and paste the copy of the pattern on the heavy cardboard.
2 Cut the cardboard horizontally across the middle on the black line.
3 Cut the lower section on the vertical line, making one piece of three toothbrush handles (**A**) and the second piece with the rest of the toothbrush handles (**B**). With the pink magic marker, color all diagonal striped toothbrush handles, and with the blue marker color the other unstriped toothbrush handles.

CHALLENGE

Placing the lower sections **A** on the left and **B** on the right, form 13 toothbrushes: 6 striped pink and 7 solid blue toothbrushes. Now switch pieces **A** and **B** to match the upper sections of the toothbrushes again. There are 7 striped pink and 6 blue color toothbrushes!
Can you figure out which toothbrush changes color?
See solution, page 46.

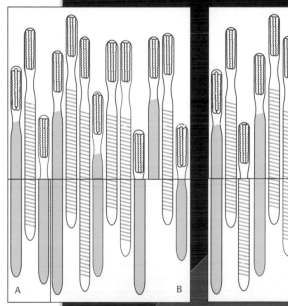
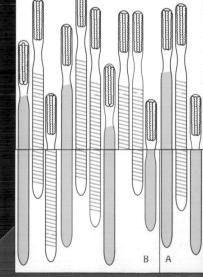

Color scheme

2–3 PRONG ILLUSION

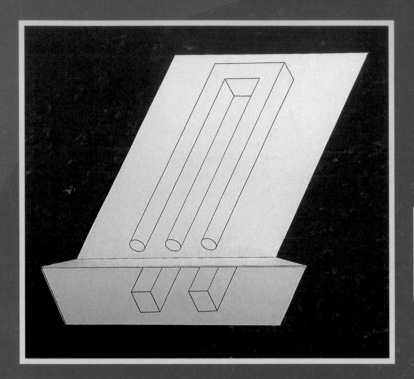

Here is a clever mechanical print of the familiar 2–3 prong optical illusion. This is a practical and simple way to make an eye-boggling effect that seems to defy what you are seeing. With the lower flap open, the three round prongs are clearly visible. Fold the lower flap on the prongs, and immediately see the two square rod-shaped prongs!

> **MATERIALS NEEDED**
> heavy paper
> 2–3 prong illusion pattern
> 5–7 light candelabra illusion pattern

CONSTRUCTION
1 Photocopy pattern A on heavy paper. Enlarge to desired size.
2 Cut on the outer lines. Fold on straight lines **ab** and **cd**.
3 Fold line **cd** (the lower flap) back and glue or tape in place, as shown. This should fold and unfold easily to show 2 or 3 prongs.

CHALLENGE
While holding the illusion, fold it toward you to cover the base. Quickly turn piece over, keeping fold in place. You have 2 prongs! **How does this happen?** See solution, page 49.

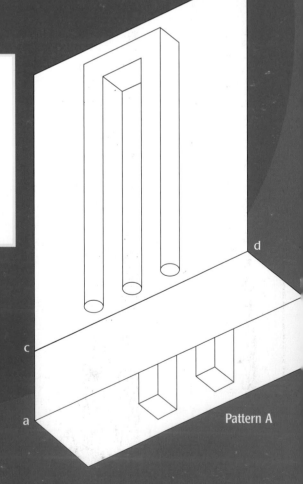

Pattern A

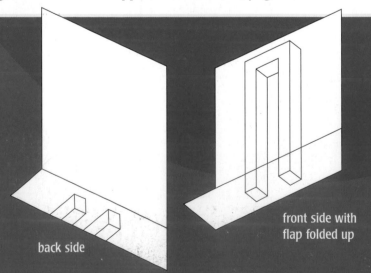

back side

front side with
flap folded up

48

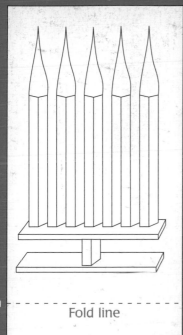

a - - - - - - - - - - - - - - - - b
Fold line

Pattern B

Solution to 2–3 Prong Illusion

For both patterns **A** and **B**, the artist fools the eye at first glance, but on close scrutiny, the long vertical lines do not really add extra prongs or lights.

EXTRA CHALLENGE

Using the same principle, a Japanese artist improved on the 2–3 prong illusion by drawing a five-light candelabra, as shown in pattern B. Enlarge and photocopy pattern B. Score and fold on line **ab**. The lower half of the drawing is covered by the fold at first, but when open, the fold reveals the entire drawing and seven lights appear on the base!

Five lights become seven by a clever artistic drawing as in the 2–3 prong illusion. Can you make six become nine using the same technique? Or make seven become ten? Try it! It's not too difficult. See solution below.

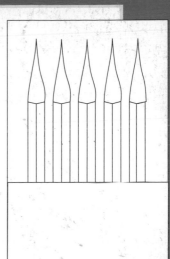

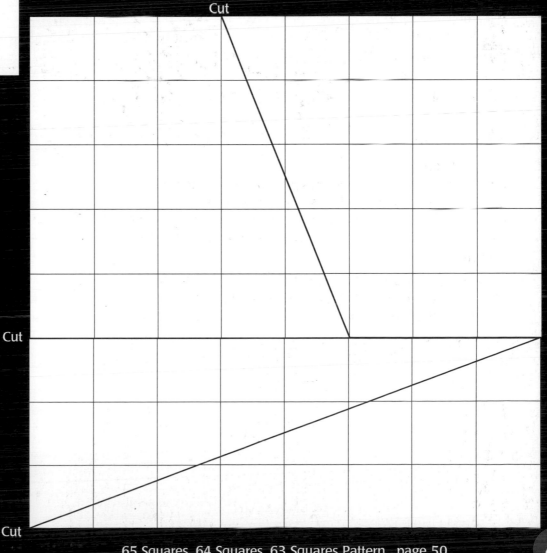

Cut

Cut

Cut

Cut

65 Squares, 64 Squares, 63 Squares Pattern , page 50

49

Most puzzles with triangles and trapezoids form a square of smaller squares, sixty-four of them. When rearranged, the pieces can form a rectangle creating sixty-five squares. The other unusual arrangement of two identical triangles and trapezoids can form not sixty-five, not sixty-four, but sixty-three squares. How can this happen?

MATERIALS NEEDED
heavy paper or cardboard
pattern, page 49
scissors
paste

CONSTRUCTION
1 Photocopy pattern on page 49 to 8 in x 8 in (20.3 cm x 20.3 cm) square.
2 Paste copy of puzzle onto heavy paper or cardboard.
3 Cut out the four pieces, as marked.

CHALLENGE 1
Arrange the four pieces to form a 5 in x 13 in (12.7 cm x 33 cm) rectangle of sixty-five squares.
Figure out how one more square was added.
See solution, page 52.

CHALLENGE 2
Arrange the four pieces so that only sixty-three squares are formed. **Figure out where the missing square has gone.**
See solution, page 52.

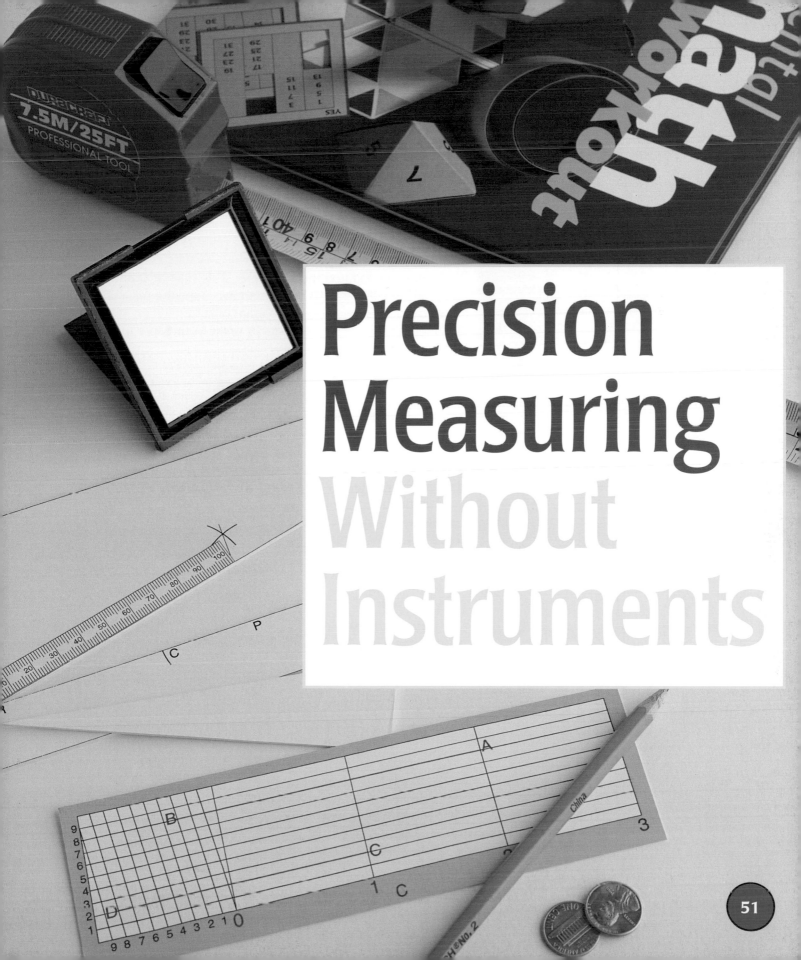

Precision
Measuring
Without
Instruments

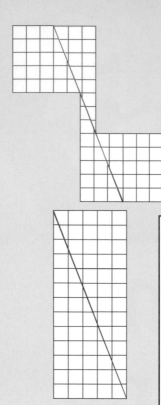

CONSTRUCTION

1 Draw line **AB** across the bottom of the card, as shown.

2 On any point on this line, construct a perpendicular line **PQ** exactly 1 in (2.5 cm) in length.

3 With compass on point **P**, mark line **AB** at points **C** and **D**. Open the compass a little larger and swing two arcs from **C** and **D** to intersect at **X** on line **P**, as shown.

4 Draw perpendicular line **XP**. (Locate point **Q** exactly 1 in or 2.5 cm from **P**.)

5 Lay the 100 point on the millimeter scale ruler at **Q** and have the 0 point touching the line **AB** at **R**, as shown. Tape the millimeter ruler to the card stock. Extend line **RQ** to edge of card.

6 Cut out this angle with scissors to make your paper micrometer, as shown.

Note The millimeter ruler must be attached to the card stock in order to read the thickness in hundredths of an inch. Example: If the round object were exactly on the hundredth line on the ruler, it would indicate $^{100}/_{100}$ of an inch or 1 inch. Anything smaller would be $^{60}/_{100}$, $^{74}/_{100}$, or any number in hundredths of an inch.

ACTIVITY

Place a pencil in the cut angle and read the millimeter number on the scale for the pencil's thickness in hundredths of an inch.
Repeat the measurement with a penny, dime, and nickel in similar manner.

CHALLENGE

Can you now figure out how to measure the inside diameter of a ring?
See solution at left.

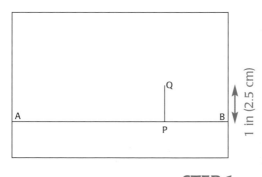

STEP 1

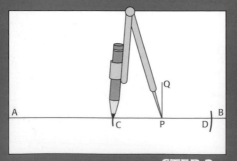

STEP 2

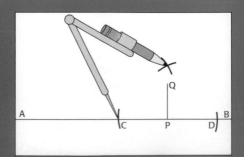

STEP 3

measuring small round objects with a
PAPER MICROMETER

Do you believe that you can measure the width of your pencil, your ring, or any coin to the nearest hundredth of an inch without precision instruments? You can with the unusual paper micrometer described below.

MATERIALS NEEDED
card stock, 4 in x 6 in (10.2 cm x 15.2 cm)
millimeter scale or old metric ruler
compass
scissors

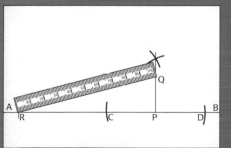

STEP 4

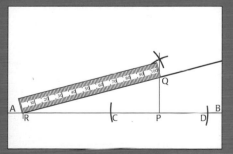

STEP 5

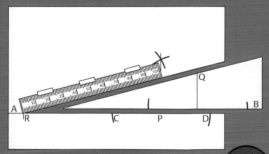

STEP 6

precise line measurement with a
DIAGONAL SCALE

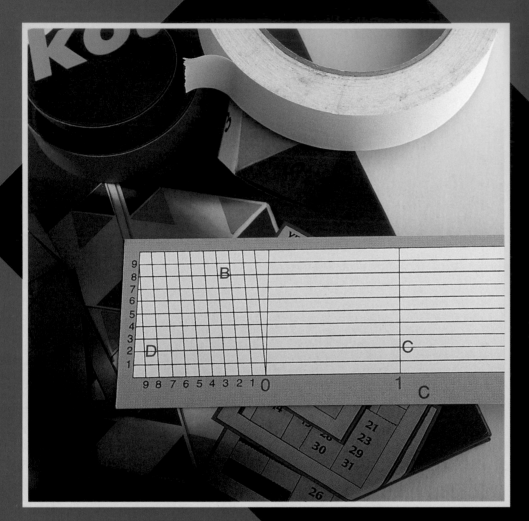

An amazing, yet simple way to accurately measure a line, a toothpick, or the thickness of a sheet of paper to one hundredth of an inch is to use a diagonal scale. This model is a practical use of a piece of geometry known as the Intercept Theorem. The same principle is used in a Diagonal Scale found on some rulers.

MATERIALS NEEDED
card stock, 2 in x 3 in (5.1 cm x 7.6 cm)
pattern
tape
pencil

CONSTRUCTION

1 Photocopy the diagonal scale onto the card stock. If longer measuring is desired, attach to a yardstick or meter stick.
Examples: Line AB represents taped pages greater than 2 in (5.1 cm) (use vertical line 2 for measuring). Line CD represents taped pages greater than 1 in (2.5 cm) (use vertical line 1 for measuring). Note For taped pages less than 1 in (2.5 cm) use vertical line 0.

CHALLENGE

Find the thickness of a page in this book using the diagonal scale card.
Hint Tape all the book pages together tightly before trying to use the scale. See solution, page 56.

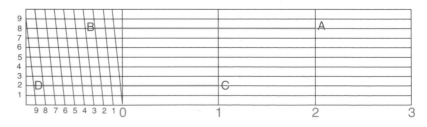

Reproduce pattern same size

measuring the height of a flagpole with a
MIRROR and YARDSTICK

In a library at Oxford, England, written in Latin during the Middle Ages, is a simple and elegant method for measuring the height of any structure without the use of trigonometry or any surveyor instruments. Translated from the Latin it reads:

Place a mirror on the ground in such a place that, when standing, you can see the reflection of the top of the object in the mirror. Now multiply the distance between the base of the object and the mirror times the height of your eyeball above the ground. Divide that answer by the distance from the mirror to your foot. The quotient is the height of the object.

MATERIALS NEEDED
pocket size mirror
yardstick or meter stick

ACTIVITY
Assume the height at the boy's eye is 5 ft (1.5 m) and the distance from his foot to the mirror is 10 ft (3 m). This ratio or comparison is the same as the height of the flagpole and the distance from the mirror to the base of the object. In this figure the distance is 30 ft (9.1 m). The simple math follows. **Can you do it?** See solution, page 56.

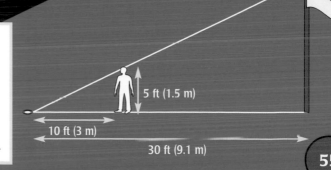

5 ft (1.5 m)

10 ft (3 m)

30 ft (9.1 m)

Math
in
Everyday
Life
Situations

Solution to Measuring the Height of a Flagpole With Mirror and Yardstick

5 is to 10 as the object height is to 30

Two comparisons
are equal fractions

$$\frac{5}{10} = \frac{height (h)}{30}$$

Solving for (h)   5 x 30 = 150.
Divide 150 by 10 = 15.
Height of object is 15 ft (4.6 m).

Solution to Precise Line Measurement With a Diagonal Scale

To find the thickness of a page of a book, tape pages tightly with masking tape, lay a straightedge along the appropriate vertical line (if the distance of the taped pages is greater than an inch, start measuring at vertical line 1; if greater than 2 inches at vertical line 2, etc.), press the taped pages against the left of the straightedge, and then place another straightedge to sandwich the pages and draw a line. Remove the book pages. Read the first number on the horizontal scale along the bottom and the second number at the intersection of the diagonal and vertical line you have drawn. Now divide the measurement obtained by the number of pages to get the thickness of a single page.

Example Assume bottom measurement is 4 and vertical measurement is 5. Add 0.4 and 0.05, so measure would be .45 in. Then divide by 90 (pages). A single page would be .005 in (.0127 cm).

THE SMART GREEK'S FORMULA
and the road builder's dilemma

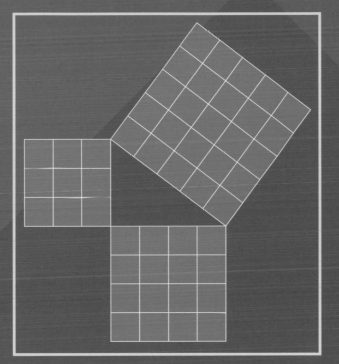

Probably the most famous theorem in math was discovered and proved by Pythagoras who said that in any right triangle, the square on the longest side (the hypotenuse) always equals the sum of the squares on the two shorter sides (the legs).

MATERIALS NEEDED
pencil
paper

As a math formula the Pythagorean theorem is stated as
c (longest side or hypotenuse) x c = a (leg) x a + b (leg) x b
or $c^2 = a^2 + b^2$

Using this formula, all math students can find any side of a right triangle if they know the lengths of the other two sides:

Example 1	Example 2
If the legs are 4 and 3, find c	If one leg is 12 and the hypotenuse is 13, find the length of leg a

Example 1
If the legs are 4 and 3, find c
$$c^2 = 4^2 + 3^2$$
$$c^2 = 16 + 9$$
$$c^2 = 25$$
$$c = \sqrt{25} \text{ or } 5$$

Example 2
If one leg is 12 and the hypotenuse is 13, find the length of leg a
$$13^2 = a^2 + 12^2$$
$169 = a^2 + 144$, then subtract 144 from each side of the equation
$$25 = a^2$$
$$\sqrt{25} \text{ or } 5 = a$$

CHALLENGE

A long, unbroken steel track, 2 miles (3.2 km) long, expands 2 ft (0.6 m) during a hot spell. A track at its center has become a serious hazard at this road crossing because the expanded track has risen a number of feet. An engineer is hired to make this crossing safe. What will he do?

The distance **AC** and **CB** are each 1 mile (5,280 ft) or 1.6 km (1609.3 m) long in normal weather. But the expanded distances **AG** and **GB** are 1 foot (0.3 m) longer (5,281 ft or 1609.6 m). The engineer uses

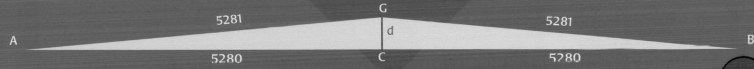

Challenge 1

Challenge 2

Solution to The Smart Greek's Formula and the Road Builder's Dilemma

The engineer didn't even consider building a ramp that needed to be over 100 ft (30.5 m) high. He simply built an underpass at road level under the track!

Solution to Two Squares Always Make a Larger Square

Challenge 1
Largest square is **APRO** with each side being ten units in length.

Challenge 2
64 sq units + 4 sq units = 68 sq units or $\sqrt{68}$ = 8.2 units (rounded)

$$c^2 = a^2 + b^2$$
$$8.2^2 = a^2 + 8^2$$
$$68 = a^2 + 64$$

Therefore $a^2 = 68 - 64 = 4$
$$a = 2$$

Solution to Solving Algebra Problems Instantly Using Geometry Card

In the previous problem Mary's time line started at six units, but now Mary's time line should start five units high. Fold from the fifth square high to the end of the base line at **C**. Fold back as in previous problem with Al's time line. The intersection of Al's and Mary's lines is the instant answer—just under 3 hours. The base line length does not affect the working of this card. It can be any longer length if you want a more precise answer.

---

the Pythagorean theorem to find **d**, which is one leg of triangle **GCB**, see diagram. Finding **d** will tell the engineer how much the tracks have risen so he can build a ramp over the road crossing.

Substituting those lengths in the formula
$$5281^2 = d^2 + 5280^2$$

$$27{,}888{,}961 = d^2 + 27{,}878{,}400$$

(subtract an equal amount from each side of the equation, i.e. −27,878,400)

$$10561 = d^2$$
$$d = \sqrt{10561} \text{ or } 102.8 \text{ ft}$$

Using metric measurements, the formula works the same:
$$1609.6^2 = d^2 + 1609.3^2$$
$$2{,}590{,}812.1 = d^2 + 2{,}589{,}846.4$$

(subtract 2,589,846.4 from each side)

$$965.7 = d^2$$
$$d = \sqrt{965.7} \text{ or } 31.1 \text{ m}$$

The amazing height of this expanded track turned out to be over 100 ft (30.5 m) above the road!

How did the road engineer solve the building of a ramp over this track?

See solution at left.

TWO SQUARES
always make a larger square

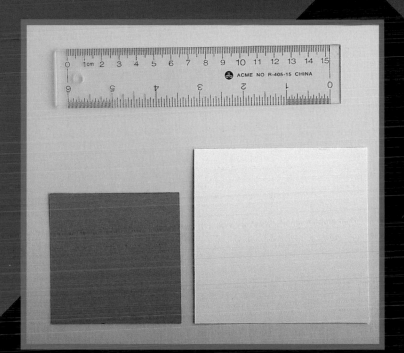

A carpenter wanted to make a square table for his workshop using two smaller square pieces of wood. There is a little known geometry idea that states that you can cut any two smaller squares in a certain way and combine them to form a perfect larger square. Do you know how to do this?

MATERIALS NEEDED
paper
pencil
metric straightedge
scissors
compass

Assume that the two smaller pieces are 8 ft x 8 ft and 6 ft x 6 ft. Draw a scale model of the two pieces on a scale of 1 cm = 1 ft, and place them together to form the figure at right.

Since the sum of the two square areas is 100 square units, the arithmetic needed for cutting them is quite simple. Since the area of the needed larger square must be 100 sq units, its side must be √100 or 10.

PROCEDURE

1 Construct right triangle **ABP**, as shown (with center at A and compass open to 10 cm, swing arc to locate point P on side a. Connect A to point P to complete triangle ABP).

2 Now use the Pythagorean theorem to find side **a** and locate point **P**, exactly.

$$c^2 = a^2 + b^2$$
$$10^2 = a^2 + 8^2$$
$$100 = a^2 + 64$$

Therefore
$$a^2 = 100 - 64 = 36$$
$$a = 6$$

Point **P** must be six units from **B** and **BP** must be six units in length.

3 Connect point **P** with the upper righthand corner of the smaller square, as shown, and mark it point **R**. This is the second leg of the larger square you are constructing. Cut along lines shown.

CHALLENGE 1

Arrange the pieces that are cut to create the larger square **APRO**.

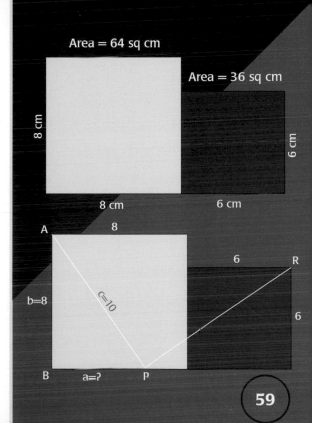

Area = 64 sq cm

Area = 36 sq cm

8 cm

6 cm

8 cm

6 cm

A   8

b=8   c=10

6   R

B   a=?   P

6

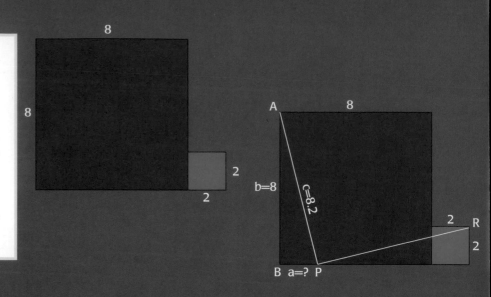

CHALLENGE 2

Let's assume one square is quite large compared to a tiny one.

Example   Square 1 is 8 x 8

                Square 2 is 2 x 2

How and where would one cut these two squares to make a perfect larger square?

Where would point P be located to construct this perfect square?

See solution, page 58.

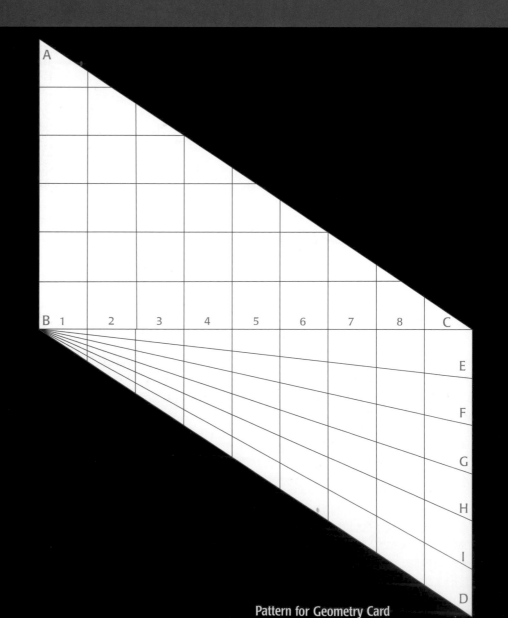

Pattern for Geometry Card

solve algebra problems instantly with
GEOMETRY CARD

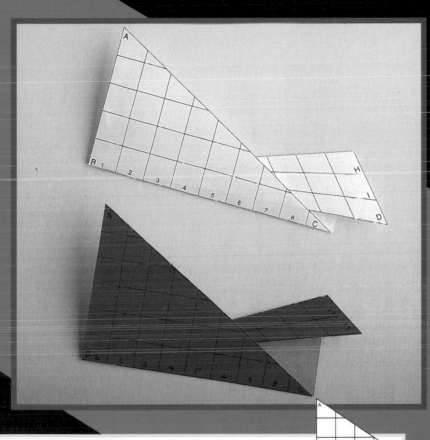

"If Mary can mow the lawn in 6 hours and Jim can mow the same lawn in 3 hours, how long will it take them to mow the same lawn if they work together?" This kind of problem, found in thousands of math books, can be annoying if you have forgotten the algebra equation and how to solve for X. Try this original folding card. It uses a simple geometry idea and gets you the answer immediately, without computer or calculator.

MATERIALS NEEDED
geometry card pattern, page 60
scissors
ballpoint pen

CONSTRUCTION

1 Photocopy the pattern on page 60.
2 Use ballpoint pen to score fold line for easy folding. Cut out the pattern as one piece.

PROCEDURE

Fold the card on base line **BC** to prepare for solving. Since Mary's mowing time is 6 hours, Line **AC** represents her working time (since AB is 6 units). Since Jim's mowing time is 3 hours, line **BG**, on lower triangle, represents his working time (since CG is 3 units). Fold back on the scored line **BG**, as shown. Fold back again on base line **BC**, as shown. The intersection of lines **BG** and **AC** gives the instant answer, which is 2.

CHALLENGE

Suppose Mary's mowing time was 5 hours, and Al's time was 6 hours. **What would be the mowing time if both worked together? Does the base line affect the working of the card?**
See solution, page 58.

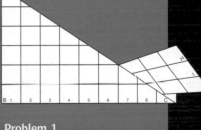

Problem 1

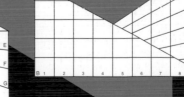

Challenge

61

HOW MANY PATHS
can you take to spell your name

This fun exercise uses the letters of your name on the triangle of squares. With short names such as Ann, Bill, Tom, and Jack, the different ways letters can be placed is rather easy. But with names with more letters such as Jennifer, Michael, and Elizabeth, the number of different ways to place the letters is quite surprising.

MATERIALS NEEDED
graph paper with ¹⁄₂ in or
   (1.3 cm) squares
scissors
markers
notebook or paper

Example: The letters F R E D on a triangle. Start with FRED along the base of the triangle, and along the height of the triangle. Would you believe there are eight ways to place the letters to spell FRED counting the two ways along the sides of the triangles?

    Start with the first F1 on the base row
        1 way

    Use second F2 on the diagonal
        3 ways

    Use third F3 on the diagonal
        3 ways

    Use fourth F4 on the diagonal
        <u>1 way</u>
        8 ways

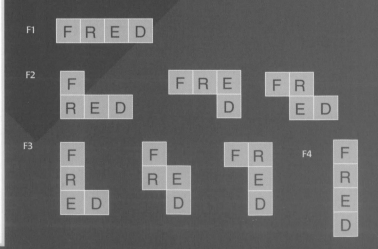

CONSTRUCTION

1 On graph paper make 5-, 6-, 7-, and 8-leg right triangles depending on the number of letters in the name you are spelling.

2 Cut out the triangles and fill in the letters of the name you are spelling. Examples shown here are DIANA and CHESTER.

CHALLENGE 1

On notepad or piece of paper, make a table (example below records paths for FRED) to record the number of paths that spell DIANA and CHESTER.

Number of letters	Number of paths starting at				Total number of paths
	F1	F2	F3	F4	
4	1	3	3	1	8

CHALLENGE 2

Can you discover a pattern as the number of letters increases?

How many letters in MATHEMATICS?

How many paths spell MATHEMATICS ?
See solutions, page 64.

Solution to **How Many Paths Can You Take to Spell Your Name?**

Number of paths for spelling Diana   16

Number of paths for spelling Chester   32

Number of paths for spelling Mathematics   1024 (11 letter word)

Number of paths for words of

5 letters	16
6 letters	32
7 letters	64
8 letters	128
9 letters	256
10 letters	512
11 letters	1024
n letters	2^{n-1}

Number of letters in word	Number of paths
2	2
3	$4 = (2 \times 2)$
4	$8 = (2 \times 4)$
5	$16 = 2^4$
6	$32 = 2^5$

Number of letters in word	Number of paths
7	$64 = 2^6$
8	$128 = 2^7$
9	$256 = 2^8$
10	$512 = 2^9$
11	$1024 = 2^{10}$

Solution to **The Many Different Paths From John's House**

The numbers in the bottom row of Pascal's Triangle are

1   10   45   120   210   252   210   120   45   10   1

Simply read the number in the box where each house is located to find the number of paths available.

The number of paths from John's house to

Ann's house—3

Mary's house—5

Ellen's house—21

Frank's house—210. It will take John 210 days, or about 7 months, to travel every path.

Solution to **Find the Area of This Unusual Garden**

Try finding the area of a 3 x 4 x 5 x 6 unit garden; then try to find the area of a 6 x 7 x 8 x 9 unit garden. Again try 8 x 9 x 10 x 11.

Instead of multiplying 3 x 4 x 5 x 6, multiply 3 x 6; then 5 x 4.

Instead of multiplying 6 x 7 x 8 x 9, multiply 6 x 9; then 7 x 8.

Instead of multiplying 8 x 9 x 10 x 11, multiply 8 x 11; then 9 x 10.

Now try our garden dimensions: instead of 7 x 8 x 9 x 10, multiply 7 x 10; then 8 x 9. There is an uncanny relationship between these products and the area of these figures. What is it?

This method of multiplying the sides of a quadrilateral yields an almost exact area if the sides are four consecutive number lengths. The rule is this: multiply the largest and smallest sides; then the two in between sides. The average of the two products is the answer. For Mr. Barnes' garden: 7 x 10 = 70; 8 x 9 = 72. Average of 70 and 72 = 71.

But as we discovered on page 67, the $\sqrt{7 \times 8 \times 9 \times 10} = \sqrt{5040}$ or 70.99 (less than 71). In fact, we also discover that as the garden gets larger, the square root of the product of the four sides is **always** less than the average of the two products (the largest x the smallest) and (the second largest x the second smallest). Example: $\sqrt{8 \times 9 \times 10 \times 11} = \sqrt{7920} = 88.99$ which is less than the average of 88 and 90 = 89. $\sqrt{9 \times 10 \times 11 \times 12} = \sqrt{11880} = 108.99$ which is less than the average of 108 and 110 = 109.

THE MANY DIFFERENT PATHS
from John's house

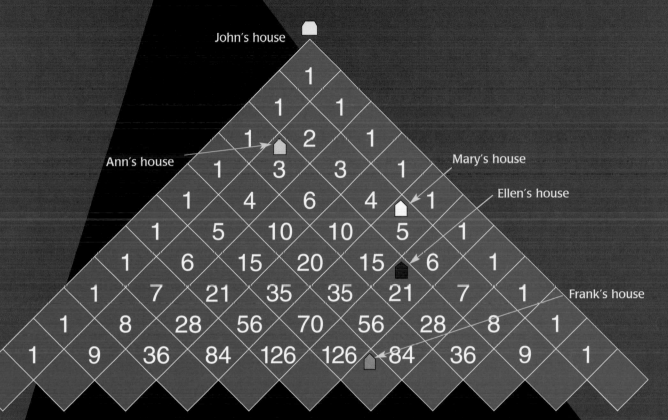

John's house

Ann's house

Mary's house

Ellen's house

Frank's house

There is a striking similarity between the many letter placements on paths to spell a name and the numbers on the famous Pascal Triangle.

MATERIALS NEEDED
paper
pencil
Pascal's Triangle pattern

CONSTRUCTION

1 Photocopy Pascal's Triangle at right.

Note the pattern. As the rows increase in size, the numbers in the rows also increase by adding the two adjacent numbers in the row above.

CHALLENGE

Complete the bottom row of Pascal's Triangle. Looking at the completed triangle, some other confusing "travel" problems can be solved instantly.

How many different ways can John take to Ann's house, or to Mary's house, or to Ellen's house?

How many months will it take John to visit Frank's house, a different way, every day, in every possible way?

See solutions, page 64.

Pascal Triangle

FIND THE AREA
of this unusual garden

Mr. Barnes has four strips of decorative fencing with which he wishes to enclose a garden. The strips are of slightly irregular lengths: 7 meters, 8 meters, 9 meters, and 10 meters. How can he arrange these strips to enclose the largest garden area possible? Although this job seems simple at first, Mr. Barnes has to do some clever arranging and figuring to prove that his arrangement gives him the largest possible garden.

MATERIALS NEEDED
stiff cardboard
ruler
pencil
utility knife
brass paper fasteners
graph paper, 1 in (2.5 cm) squares

CONSTRUCTION

1 Using scale of 1 in (2.5 cm) = 1 meter, measure and cut four strips of stiff cardboard in 7, 8, 9, and 10 inch lengths.

2 Attach the four strips with brass fasteners to form a quadrilateral (4-sided shape). Experiment with the fencing strips and see if you can discover and prove what is the largest garden possible. Obviously the problem could be solved simply if a perfect square could be formed, but the unequal lengths prevent this. One logical approach is to form as many square corners as possible.

Hint A 7 in x 9 in rectangle can be formed within the quadrilateral, but two sections of it to the right and below the rectangle are protruding and have to be accounted for. They are difficult to measure and compute.

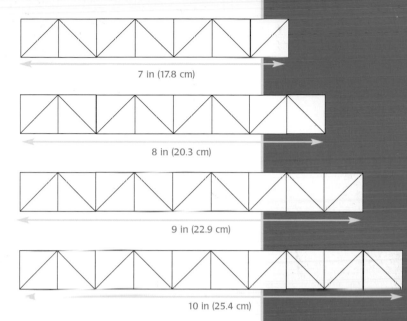

7 in (17.8 cm)

8 in (20.3 cm)

9 in (22.9 cm)

10 in (25.4 cm)

Another way to obtain the garden area is to divide each of these figures into two triangles, then add their areas. This method is not easy, either. Is there a better way?

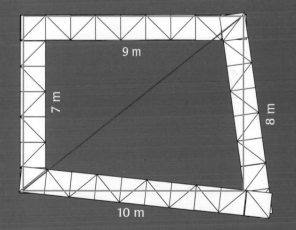

9 m

7 m

8 m

10 m

Using all right angles, the blue rectangle is possible

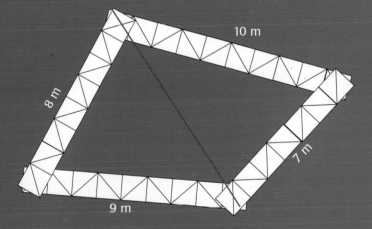

10 m

8 m

7 m

9 m

Creating no right angles is much more difficult to calculate the area

CHALLENGE

The model above on the left shows a 7 x 9 rectangle outlined in blue, and its area is not so difficult to compute. However, the two overlapping triangles are quite difficult to measure.

We know that a rectangular garden enclosed by two 8 m and two 10 m strips would yield a maximum area because of the right angles formed. Instead of the simple height x base formula, there is an unusual area formula that also works: multiply all sides and find the square root of the product—8 x 10 x 8 x 10 = 6400; then finding the square root of 6400 produces the area of 80 sq m.

Applying this method to the quadrilateral garden: 7 x 8 x 9 x 10 = 5040. The square root of 5040 produces an area of 70.99. For all practical purposes 70.99 can be rounded to 71 square units.

Can you prove that $\sqrt{7 \times 8 \times 9 \times 10}$ is less than 71? See solution on page 64.

Solitaire
Games

LUCKY SEVEN

Board Pattern

This game seems simple enough but takes planning-ahead strategy to solve the challenge. Whether you are eight or eighty years of age, the task is the same. In seven moves or jumps, you are to remove fifteen pegs leaving the colored one alone at the end.

MATERIALS NEEDED
block of wood, 9 in x 4 in x ¾ in (22.9 cm x 10.2 cm x 1.9 cm) thick
3 in (7.6 cm) dowel, ³⁄₁₆ in (0.5 cm) thick
¼ in (0.6 cm) drill
sandpaper
board pattern
markers

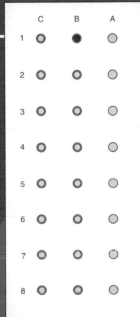

CONSTRUCTION
1 Make a copy of the board pattern above. Enlarge copy as required.
2 Using the diagram as a template, drill three rows of ³⁄₁₆ in (0.5 cm) holes in the block of wood.
3 Cut sixteen 1½ in (3.8 cm) dowels from the dowel piece.
4 Make one dowel a distinctive color and place at the beginning of the center row (B).

CHALLENGE
With all dowels in place and the distinctive one at the beginning of row B, the objective is to remove all the other pegs in seven moves. One jump, whether single, double, triple, or more, constitutes one move, as in a game of checkers. Jumps may be made horizontally, vertically, or diagonally. Pegs are removed after each jump. Moving a peg one space to facilitate a move also counts as a move. The distinctive peg must remain alone after seven moves to successfully complete the challenge. See solution, page 72.
Hint Plan ahead with the first few moves for multiple jumps later.

TWENTY TRIANGLES
make a perfect square

Using a little logical math thinking and twenty identical triangular pieces you can arrange them in an orderly fashion to construct a perfect square. You can also make many shapes and figures using all twenty pieces, but the square will give you the greatest feeling of achievement.

> **MATERIALS NEEDED**
> heavy poster board or thin plywood
> bond paper
> saw or sharp knife
> sandpaper

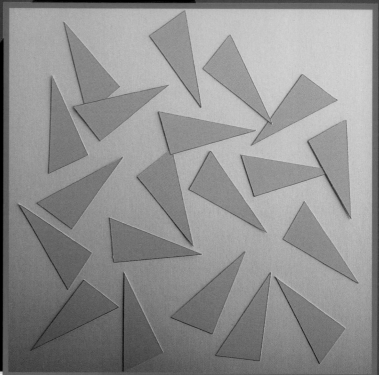

CONSTRUCTION

1 Using bond paper construct template of right triangle, as shown, with altitude of 1 in and base of 2 in. If you prefer metric measurements use altitude of 3 cm and base of 6 cm.

2 Trace the template on poster board or plywood twenty times to form twenty right triangles, as shown. Cut triangles with a saw or knife. Sand if needed.

Note An easy way to cut the twenty triangles is to first cut a 4 in x 5 in rectangle. Divide the 5-in sides into five one-inch strips, as shown. Divide the 4 in sides in half with center line 2 in from top and bottom of rectangle. Then divide this center line into five one-inch segments and construct diagonals, as shown.

CHALLENGE

Using all twenty pieces, form a perfect square.

Hint The area of one triangular piece is 1 sq in. Placing the pieces in random order can be quite difficult. However, there is a clever way to simplify this challenge.

Can you figure what the total area of this square must be and what the length of the side of this square must be?
See solution, page 72.

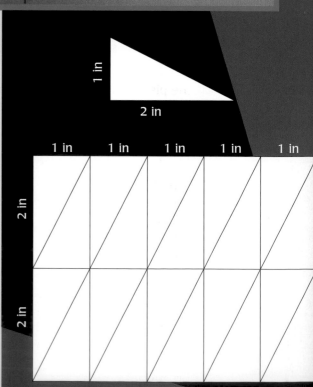

70

MOVING NINE PENNIES
in nine moves

Moving nine pennies to the shaded area on the board is an easy task if you are allowed ten or eleven moves, but to make the transfer in nine moves is not so easy. Try it and see!

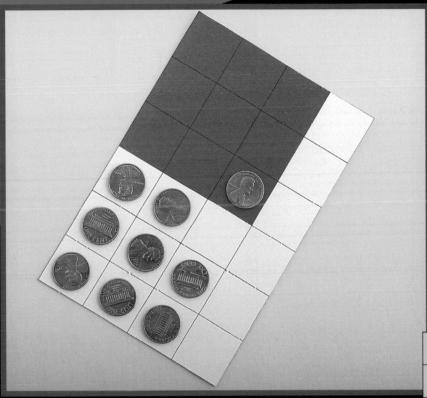

MATERIALS NEEDED
heavy cardboard, $4\frac{1}{2}$ in x $6\frac{7}{8}$ in
    (11.4 cm x 17.5 cm)
ruler
marker
9 pennies

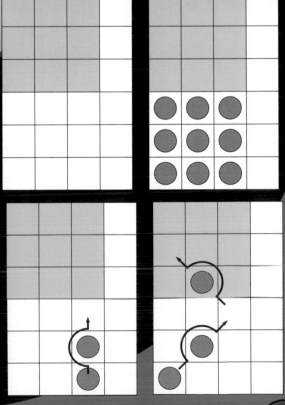

CONSTRUCTION

1 Using the piece of cardboard, $4\frac{1}{2}$ in x $6\frac{7}{8}$ in (11.4 cm x 17.5 cm) measure a six by four array of squares that are approximately $1\frac{1}{8}$ in (2.9 cm) square, as shown.
2 Using the marker, shade the nine upper left squares.

CHALLENGE

Place a penny on each of the nine squares, as shown. Your task is to move all nine pennies up to the nine shaded squares while observing the following rules:
1 You may move a penny to any empty square in any direction up, down, right, left, or diagonally.
2 You may jump over any penny in any direction to an empty square and you may continue jumping as many times as you like if the pattern permits, as shown. A chain of jumps counts as one move.

What is the fewest number of moves required to transfer all nine pennies to the shaded area?
See solution, page 72.

Solution to Lucky Seven

Starting position: Pegs in rows B and C; Row A holes are empty.

1. 3C jumps 3B; lands on 3A
2. 5C jumps 5B; lands on 5A
3. 7C jumps 7B; lands on 7A
4. 8C jumps 8B, 7A, 5A, and 3A; lands on 2A
5. 1C jumps 2C, 4C, 6C then diagonally 6B, 4B, 2B, and finally 2A; lands on 3A
6. 1B moves diagonally to 2A
7. 2A jumps 3A

Solution to Twenty Triangles Make a Perfect Square

If the area of one of the triangles is 1 sq in, obviously all twenty triangles must form an area of 20 sq in. The length of the side of this square must be the square root of twenty or two times the square root of five $(2\sqrt{5})$.

Using the Pythagorean theorem, the length of the hypotenuse of one triangular piece is the square root of the sums of the squares of the two legs, or smaller sides of the triangle. The mathematical formula is: $c^2 = a^2 + b^2$.

For this triangle: c^2 (hypotenuse²) $= 1^2 + 2^2$, or $1 + 4$, or 5.

Since $c^2 = 5$, then $c = \sqrt{5}$. This means that the hypotenuse is the square root of 5, that means it is half the length of the side of the square being formed. Therefore, two of the longest sides of each piece will form a side of the square, and eight of them will form the outer boundary of the square we are constructing. The other twelve pieces will easily fit inside, as shown.

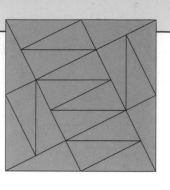

Solution to Moving Nine Pennies in Nine Moves

The transfer of pennies can be done in nine moves. Numbers identify each penny and trace each movement. The six by four array is necessary to make the eighth move for penny number 5.

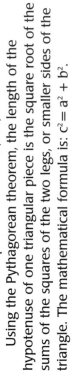

Move sequence

Solution to The Buffon Toothpick Experiment

Here is a simplified proof of the Buffon toothpick experiment. The approximate comparison of the number of times a toothpick will contact a line with the times a toothpick will not touch a line can be seen on the simple graph, shown here. (Note Exact proof can be determined by calculus.)

The closer the toothpick falls perpendicular to a line the greater the chance of touching the line. In simple terms, the rectangle represents all the tosses. The larger area under the curve represents "number of contacts." The smaller area represents "no contacts."

The more tosses tabulated, the closer one comes to the approximate value of π.

My results of this experiment are: 50 tosses (T) with 28 contacts (C), or $2 \times \dfrac{50}{28} = \dfrac{100}{28} = 3.5+$

100 tosses (T) with 60 contacts (C), or $2 \times \dfrac{100}{60} = \dfrac{200}{60} = 3.3+$

150 tosses (T) with 93 contacts (C), or $2 \times \dfrac{150}{93} = \dfrac{300}{93} = 3.1+$

Tosses that do not contact the line

Tosses that contact the line (C)

Note the rule π **almost** $= 2 \times$ No. of tosses (T) divided by No. of tosses that contact the line (C) = 3.1416+.
Louis Buffon, with his toothpicks, certainly discovered a most unusual and amazing way to arrive at the value of π.

BUFFON TOOTHPICK EXPERIMENT

About 200 years ago, Louis Buffon, intrigued with finding the value of π, tried an experiment dropping toothpicks, thousands of times, on a lined surfaced. He arrived at a formula (rule) that came closer to the value of π the more times he dropped his toothpicks on the line surface. The rule was that π was almost equal to twice the number of toothpicks dropped divided by the number of toothpicks that touched the line. Written as a mathematical rule π = 2 x (number of tosses divided by number of tosses that touched a line).

The most amazing result of simply dropping toothpicks on these lines was that the more toothpicks dropped the closer his rule proved to reach the value of π that computers had determined.

CONSTRUCTION

1 Measure the length of toothpicks.
2 Using pencil and ruler, mark points on the large sheet of paper to make parallel lines exactly the distance apart as the length of the toothpicks. Parallel lines should fill the entire sheet of paper. See photograph.
3 Fasten the lined sheet of paper to a flat surface or table.

EXPERIMENT

1 Drop toothpicks one by one from a circular bowl about 3 ft (0.9 m) above the lined paper that has been fastened to a flat surface or table.
2 Set up a table to record the experiment data. For example:

Number of tosses (T)	1st	2nd	3rd, etc.
Tosses that contact a line (C)	x		x
Tosses not contacting a line		x	
C/T	1/1	1/2	2/3
2 x T/C	2	4	3

What is the value of π after 50 tosses? After 100 tosses? After 500 tosses?

Does your experiment perform as Louis Buffon demonstrated?

Can you guess why his rule is twice the comparison of tosses and touches?

Japanese very different
TANGRAMS

Unlike the Chinese puzzle of ancient times this Japanese Tangram version called Ingenious Pieces by Sei Shonagon is quite new but offers a clever square-hole puzzle and some designs and shapes to construct for fun and challenge. This set of tans can be made easily from thin plywood or heavy cardboard and is an ideal, original pastime for birthday parties or group contests.

CONSTRUCTION

1 Using paper cutter or saw, cut a 5 in (12.7 cm) square from heavy cardboard or thin plywood.
2 Cut square in half, diagonally, as shown.
3 Locate the midpoints of the sides of both triangles: **a**, **b**, **c**, **d**
4 Cut along lines **ab** and **cd** to form triangles **I** and **II**.
5 Locate midpoints **e**, **f**, and **g**.
6 Cut **ef** to form trapezoid **III**.
7 Cut **hg** parallel to right side to form parallelogram **IV** and trapezoid **V**.
8 Cut **cj** parallel to **ef** to form square **VI** and triangle **VII**.

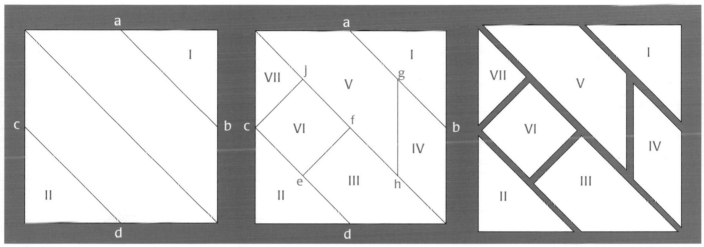

ACTIVITY

1 Form a square with all pieces and the small square off center in two ways. (Easy)
2 Form a square with these seven pieces and with a square in the center. (Tricky!)
3 Form these geometric shapes: rectangle, right triangle, parallelogram, trapezoid, hexagon and pentagon.

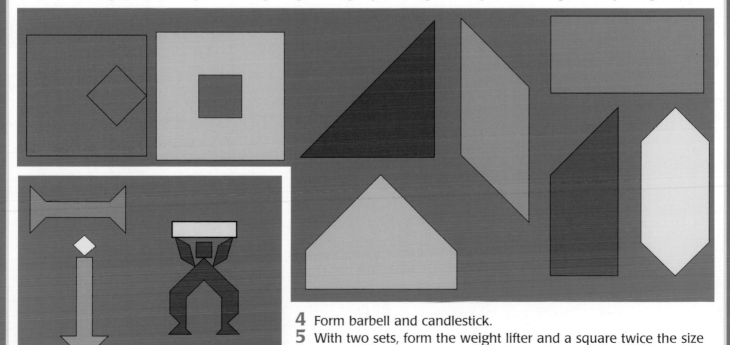

4 Form barbell and candlestick.
5 With two sets, form the weight lifter and a square twice the size of the original square. See solutions, page 76.

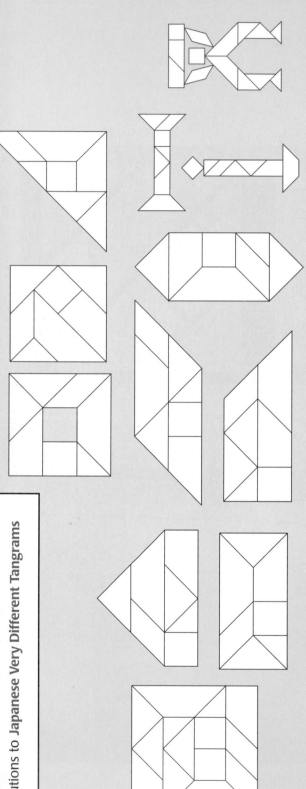

Solutions to Japanese Very Different Tangrams

Solutions to **Make a Square With Only Five Pieces**
Challenge

Extra Challenge

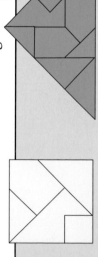

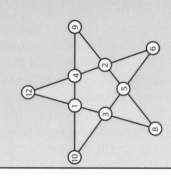

Solution to **Create a Perfect Star and Play the Numbers Game**

Begin by writing the five smallest numbers on the gummy labels at the intersection points of the inner pentagon, in a random manner: 1, 2, 3, 4, and 5. The sum of these is 15, but since they are used twice, they account for thirty of the 120 (24 x 5) total of the five lines. This means that the other five numbers on the points of the star, each used twice on different lines, must account for 90 (120 – 30). With trial and error (move about numbered gummy labels) you soon discover that the 11 and 7 pair can be eliminated, leaving 6, 8, 9, 10, and 12 whose total is 45, which when used twice and doubled, equals 90.

You know that five lines, each with a value of 24, make a total of 5 x 24 or 120. But since each number is a part of two lines and used twice to make a total of 120, then the sum of the numbers added once must be 60. However, one can easily see that the sum of the series: 1, 2, 3, 4, 5, 6, 7, 8, 9, 10, 11, 12 is 78. Therefore, to use ten numbers that total 60, you must eliminate two of the twelve numbers that total 18. (78 – 18 = 60). There are only three pairs that add to 18: 12 and 6, 11 and 7, and 10 and 8. One of these pairs must not be used.

MAKE A SQUARE
with only five pieces

Arranging and rearranging these five pieces, you might think it's impossible to make a square. But with ingenuity, it really can be done. Furthermore, with two sets of similar pieces (10 pieces) you can make the other three basic geometric shapes: a perfect triangle, a rectangle, and a pentagon.

MATERIALS NEEDED
heavy cardboard or thin plywood
utility knife or saw
sandpaper
pencil

CONSTRUCTION
1 Photocopy the five pattern pieces, enlarging to desired size. Cut out.
2 Trace pattern pieces onto cardboard or thin plywood.
3 Cut with utility knife or saw.
4 Sand any rough edges.
5 Make two sets of five pieces.

CHALLENGE
Construct a perfect square using all five pieces.

EXTRA CHALLENGE
Construct the rectangle, triangle, and pentagon, using two sets of pieces, ten in all.
Hint   You can reverse the pieces.
See solutions, page 76.

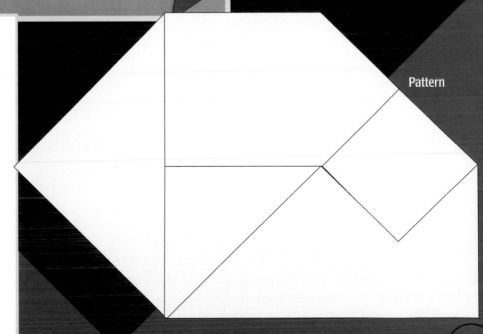

Pattern

77

CREATE A PERFECT STAR
and play the numbers game

Construct a pentagon using no protractor and no ruler and a perfect star (pentagram) magically appears. Then play the magic number game using ten numbers from this series: 1, 2, 3, 4, 5, 6, 7, 8, 9, 10, 11, and 12. (Note two of the twelve numbers are not used.) The sum of the numbers along each of five lines is 24. With some planning and a little trial and error, this magic star with 24 units to each line can be created with the smallest and most interesting sum.

MATERIALS NEEDED
heavy paper strip, 3 in x 24 in (7.6 cm x 61 cm)
sheet of bond paper
scissors
tape or glue
gummy labels

CONSTRUCTION

1 Fold the paper strip into a knot, as you would a rope, and then fold and crease carefully to make a pentagon, as shown.

2 Draw a line from each vertex to the two opposite corners, as shown, to form a star.

3 Cut the five unmarked triangle pieces, as indicated.

4 Tape or glue the five points to the bond paper to make the star figure more stable.

5 Place labels on star, as shown.

CHALLENGE

Using ten of the numbers in the twelve-number series, make this magical pentagram, so that the four numbers assigned to each label in a line totals 24.

Hint How many times is each single number a part of a line?

What will the sum of all the line totals be?
See solution, page 76.

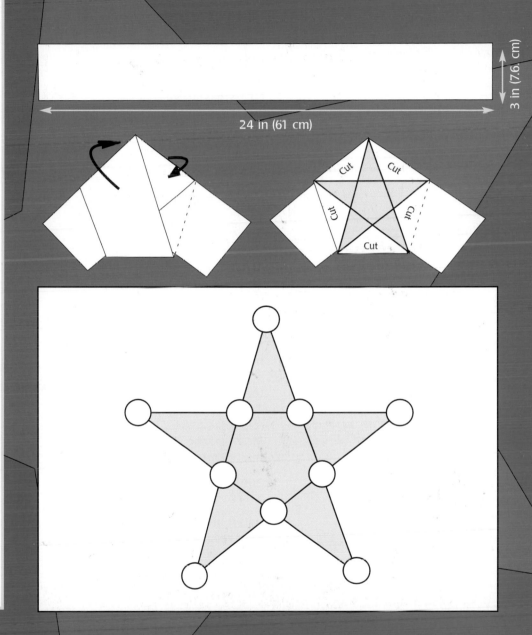

24 in (61 cm)

3 in (7.6 cm)

Cut Cut Cut Cut Cut

Index

adding five items, 41, 42
addition triangle, 30, 31, 32
aestheometry, 6
age guessing, 27
algebra problems, 61
amazing number 143, 24–25
amazing number 429, 26

Buffon, Louis, 73
Buffon Toothpick Experiment, 72, 73

card trick, 30–31, 32
charm cards, 35–36
charm card patterns, 35
checkers-like game, 69
choose your fortune, 34–37, 38
color-changing miracle, 46, 47
concentric circles, 9
Confident Gambler, 28–29, 32
Create a Perfect Star, 76, 78–79
cyclic number, 39

Diagonal Scale, 54, 56
diagonal scale card, 54
dollar signs, 44, 45, 46

flexatube, 20–22
Floating Sphere, 6–8
floating sphere stringing, 7, 8
floating sphere pattern, 8
fortune telling, 34
fortune telling charm list, 37

garden area puzzle, 64, 66, 67
geometrical design, 6
geometry card, 58, 60, 61
geometry card solves algebra problems, 58, 61

hexaflexagon, 13–15
hexaflexagon flexing, 15
how many paths to spell your name, 62–63, 64
how many paths from John's house, 64, 65
Hyakugo Gen, 27

Ingenious Pieces, 74
Intercept theorem, 54

introduction, 4
Japanese tangrams, 74–75, 76

king's problem, 33

Lightning Addition, 40, 42
line measurement, 54
Lucky Seven, 69, 72
Lucky Seven board pattern, 69

magical shapes, 16–17
magical shapes pattern, 17
make a larger square from two smaller squares, 59, 60
make a square with five pieces, 76, 77
make-a-square puzzle, 50, 52
measuring flagpoles, 55, 56
measuring small round objects, 52–53
measuring with mirror and yardstick, 55, 56
mind reading, 28, 29, 34, 38
missing dollar puzzle, 44, 45, 46
missing dollar puzzle pattern A, 44
missing dollar puzzle pattern B, 44
missing squares, 49, 50, 52
Moving Nine Pennies, 71, 72
multiply by cutting a strip, 39

numbers game creates a star, 76, 78–79

odd-numbered problem, 33
oranges for sale, 45, 46
optical illusions, 48, 49

paper micrometer, 52, 53
paperweight, 18, 22
Pascal's Triangle, 65
paths to John's house, 64, 65
playing cards, 29, 31, 32, 33
pyramids, 16
Pythagorean theorem, 57, 58

road-builder's dilemma, 57, 58

shopping list, 41

Shonagon, Sei, 74
65 Squares, 64 Squares, 63 Squares, 50
65 squares, 64 squares, 63 squares pattern, 49
smart Greek's formula, 57, 58
space mathematics, 6
spelling paths, 62, 63, 64
split-second multiplication, 39
stadium design from concentric circles, 9–12
stadium design pattern, 12
stadium design stringing sequence, 10, 11
star creation, 76, 78–79

tangrams, 74–75, 76
tetraflexagon, 13–15
tetrahedron, 18–19, 22
tetrahedron pattern, 19
toothbrush changes color, 46, 47
toothbrush changes color pattern, 46
toothpick experiment, 73
top card prediction, 32
trapezoids, 44, 45, 50
Twenty Triangles Make a Square, 70, 72
2-3 Prong Illusion, 48, 49
2-3 prong illusion pattern A, 48
2-3 prong illusion pattern B, 49
two squares make one square, 59, 60

value of π, 73

wall hanging, 9